SICILY TRAVEL GUIDE

2024-2025

Unveiling Adventures, Culinary Delights, Rich History, Cozy Accommodation and Hidden Gems

Alex Fowler

Copyright © by Alex Fowler 2024.

All rights reserved.

Except for brief quotations used in critical reviews and other non-commercial uses permitted by copyright law, no part of this publication may be copied, distributed, or transmitted in any way without the publisher's prior written consent, including by photocopying, recording, or other electronic or mechanical methods.

The use of any trademarks or brands mentioned in this book is solely for the purpose of clarification and is not intended to imply any affiliation with the respective owners of those marks or brands.

Map of Sicily

[Click here to View the Map of Sicily](#) (For e-book readers)

Scan the QR Code below with your mobile phone's Camera to View the Map of Sicily (For Paperback Readers).

TABLE OF CONTENTS

Map of Sicily

INTRODUCTION

    History of Sicily

CHAPTER 1

Planning Your Trip

    Best Times to Visit

    Cultural Etiquette

    Essential Sicilian Phrases

CHAPTER 2

Travel Essentials

    Visa Requirements

    Travel Insurance

    Health and Safety Tips

CHAPTER 3

Getting There and Around

    Arriving in Sicily: Airports and Entry Points

    Local Transportation: From Scooters to Buses

CHAPTER 4

Accommodation Options

    Luxury Resorts

    Mid-range Hotels

    Budget Stays and Hostels

    Unique Accommodations: Agrotourism and Historical Stays

CHAPTER 5
Top Attractions
    Historical Landmarks
    Natural Wonders
    Museums and Galleries
CHAPTER 6
Hidden Gems
    Off-the-Beaten-Path Destinations
    Lesser-Known Beaches
    Local Markets and Shops
CHAPTER 7
Things to Do
    As a Solo Traveler
    For Couples: Romantic Escapes
    With Kids: Family-Friendly Activities
    As a Family: Group Adventures
    As a Senior Traveler
    Outdoor Activities: Hiking, Sailing, and More
CHAPTER 8
Dining and Nightlife
    Traditional Sicilian Cuisine
    Best Restaurants for Every Budget
    Nightlife: Bars and Live Music Venues
CHAPTER 9
Cultural Experiences
    Festivals and Events

    Cooking Classes and Wine Tasting

    Historical Tours

CHAPTER 10

Practical Information

    Currency, Banking, and ATMs

    Connectivity: SIM Cards and Internet Access

    Emergency Contacts and Useful Numbers

CHAPTER 11

Packing List

    Seasonal Packing Tips

    Must-Have Items for Sicily

CHAPTER 12

Itineraries

    Day Trips and Excursions

    3-Day Itineraries

    7-Day Itineraries

CHAPTER 13

Helpful Resources

    The Geography of Sicily

    The Climate of Sicily

    Car Rentals and Navigating on Your Own

    Guided Tours: Options and Recommendations

    Useful Apps and Websites for Travel in Sicily

CONCLUSION

INTRODUCTION

Sicily, the largest island in the Mediterranean, stands as a crossroads of cultures, history, and gastronomy. Its strategic location just off the southern tip of Italy's mainland has made it a pivotal point of convergence for numerous civilizations, including the Greeks, Romans, Normans, and Arabs. Each of these cultures has left an indelible mark, contributing to the rich tapestry that defines Sicilian heritage today.

This travel guide aims to be your comprehensive companion as you explore the depths of Sicily's treasures. From the archaeological ruins that whisper tales of ancient times to the bustling markets redolent with the fresh scents of local produce and seafood, this book promises to guide you through an array of enriching experiences. Navigating Sicily might seem daunting, but this guide will simplify your travel plans. We provide detailed insights into the various transport options available, whether you prefer to drive, use public transport, or explore on foot. Accommodations are plentiful and varied, with options ranging from luxurious hotels to charming bed and breakfasts that offer a personal touch and a taste of local life. Cuisine in Sicily is not just food; it's a cultural expression rooted in centuries of history and influenced by all those who have walked its lands. Here, you will learn where to sample traditional dishes like pasta alla Norma and caponata, and where to find the best cannoli, ensuring each meal enriches your travel experience.

To assist you in planning a smooth trip, this guide includes practical advice covering essential topics such as up-to-date visa requirements, safety tips, and packing suggestions. It caters to various types of travelers—whether you are on a solo journey, traveling as a couple, adventuring with kids, or exploring with friends. We provide tailored suggestions to help you make the most of your Sicilian adventure.

As you delve into the subsequent chapters, you will uncover not only the iconic sites and hidden gems of Sicily but also engage with the spirit of the island. Our aim is for you to not just visit Sicily, but to experience it fully, immersing yourself in its vibrant culture, stunning landscapes, and historical wonders. Your journey through Sicily starts here, unfolding a path of discovery that promises both the excitement of exploration and the comfort of learning. Let this guide be your gateway to an unforgettable adventure in one of the Mediterranean's most captivating destinations.

History of Sicily

The history of Sicily is rich and complex, marked by a series of conquests and cultural influences that have shaped the island into what it is today. Sicily's story begins in prehistoric times when it was inhabited by ancient tribes like the Sicani, Elymians, and Sicels. These indigenous groups left behind traces of their existence in the form of tools, pottery, and cave paintings.

Around the 8th century BC, the island saw the arrival of Greek settlers who established colonies such as Syracuse, Agrigento, and Catania. The Greeks introduced their language, art, and architecture, leaving a lasting legacy. Many of Sicily's famous archaeological sites, like the Valley of the Temples in Agrigento, are remnants of this period. The Greeks also brought their religious practices, with temples dedicated to gods like Zeus and Apollo. In the 3rd century BC, the island fell under the control of the Roman Republic after the Punic Wars with Carthage.

Sicily became the first Roman province outside the Italian Peninsula. Under Roman rule, Sicily flourished as an agricultural hub, producing grain, olives, and wine for the empire. The Romans also built impressive structures, including villas, theaters, and aqueducts, some of which can still be seen today.

Following the fall of the Roman Empire in the 5th century AD, Sicily experienced a period of turmoil and change. The island was invaded by various groups, including the Vandals and the Ostrogoths, before becoming part of the Byzantine Empire in the 6th century. Byzantine rule introduced Eastern Orthodox Christianity to the island and left behind beautiful mosaics and churches.

In the 9th century, Arab forces from North Africa conquered Sicily. The Arabs, or Moors, ruled for over two centuries, transforming the island's culture, economy, and architecture. They introduced advanced agricultural techniques, new crops like citrus fruits, and the intricate designs seen in many buildings. The Arab influence is also evident in the island's language and cuisine.

The Norman conquest of Sicily began in the 11th century. Led by Roger I, the Normans gradually took control of the island, establishing the Kingdom of Sicily in 1130. The Normans were known for their tolerance of different cultures and religions, creating a unique blend of Norman, Arab, and Byzantine influences. This period saw the construction of impressive cathedrals and palaces, such as the Cathedral of Monreale and the Palazzo dei Normanni in Palermo.

The subsequent centuries saw Sicily under the rule of various European powers, including the Hohenstaufen, Angevins, and Aragonese. Each of these rulers left their mark on the island's culture and architecture. In the late 15th century, Sicily became part of the Spanish Empire, leading to further cultural exchange and development.

The 19th century brought significant change with the unification of Italy. Sicily played a crucial role in the Risorgimento, the movement for Italian unification, and became part of the newly formed Kingdom of Italy in 1861. However, the island faced economic challenges and social unrest during this period, leading to waves of emigration.

The 20th century was marked by the impact of World War II, during which Sicily was a key battleground. The Allied invasion of Sicily in 1943 was a turning point in the war, leading to the eventual downfall of Mussolini's regime. After the war, Sicily became an autonomous region within the Italian Republic, allowing for greater self-governance. Today, Sicily's rich history is evident in its diverse cultural heritage, from ancient Greek temples and Roman amphitheaters to Arab-Norman architecture and Baroque churches. The island's history is a tapestry woven with the threads of many civilizations, each contributing to the unique character of Sicily. Understanding this history provides valuable insight into the island's identity and its enduring appeal as a destination for travelers from around the world.

CHAPTER 1

Planning Your Trip

This chapter will guide you through all the essentials you need to consider before you start your journey, making sure you're well-prepared and informed.

Firstly, it's important to pick the best time to visit. Sicily enjoys a Mediterranean climate, meaning hot, dry summers and mild, wet winters. Depending on what you want to do, some seasons might suit your plans better than others. For beach lovers, summer is ideal, while those interested in hiking or exploring the towns without the heat might prefer the cooler months. Understanding local travel options will also be crucial.

This chapter will cover the different ways you can move around Sicily. Whether you prefer renting a car to explore at your own pace, or using public transport like buses and trains, knowing your options will help you travel more smoothly and enjoyably.

Accommodations in Sicily range from luxurious hotels to cozy, family-run guesthouses. We'll discuss how to choose the best place to stay based on your budget and travel style. Whether you're looking for a place near the beach, a quiet retreat in the countryside, or a vibrant spot in the city center, you'll find useful tips here. Finally, we'll touch on some practical matters such as travel insurance, health tips, and safety advice. While Sicily is generally a safe destination, it's always wise to be prepared for any situation that might arise.

This chapter aims to arm you with all the information you need to plan an enjoyable and hassle-free trip to Sicily. By the end of it, you'll feel ready and excited to start your adventure in one of the most enchanting regions of Italy.

Best Times to Visit

Choosing the best time to visit Sicily can greatly enhance your experience, depending on what you want to see and do. Sicily is a beautiful destination with a Mediterranean climate, characterized by hot, dry summers and mild, wet winters. This climate affects when might be the best time for you to visit.

If you enjoy warm weather and sunny skies, the summer months from June to August are ideal. During this period, the temperatures are typically high, often climbing above 30 degrees Celsius (86 degrees Fahrenheit). This is perfect for beach-goers who want to soak up the sun and enjoy the crystal-clear waters of the Mediterranean. However, it's worth noting that this is also the peak tourist season. Beaches, landmarks, and tourist spots can be very crowded, and prices for accommodations and activities can rise due to high demand.

For those who prefer a more relaxed visit with fewer crowds, the spring (April to June) and autumn (September to November) months are excellent choices. The weather during these months is generally mild and pleasant, making it ideal for exploring outdoor sites and wandering through ancient towns. In spring, the countryside is vibrant with colorful flowers and green landscapes, while autumn offers the chance to experience local harvests, including grapes, olives, and various fruits. These seasons are particularly good for those interested in outdoor activities like hiking, as the cooler temperatures make for more comfortable conditions.

Winter in Sicily, from December to February, is the quietest tourist period. The weather is cooler and can be unpredictable, with some rainy days, but temperatures rarely drop below 10 degrees Celsius (50 degrees Fahrenheit). This time of year offers a unique opportunity to explore Sicilian culture without the crowds. Coastal areas are quieter, and you can enjoy the beauty of snow-capped mountains if you venture into higher elevations like the areas around Mount Etna. Winter is also an excellent time for those interested in cultural events and festivals, which are abundant during the Christmas and Carnival seasons.

Ultimately, the best time to visit Sicily depends on your personal preferences and what you hope to get out of your trip. Whether it's lounging on the beaches in the heat of summer, enjoying the spring blooms, experiencing the harvest in autumn, or exploring the cultural events in winter, Sicily has something to offer in every season. By considering what each time of year offers, you can plan a trip that aligns with your interests and provides the most rewarding experience.

Cultural Etiquette

Understanding cultural etiquette in Sicily is essential for any visitor aiming to respect and engage meaningfully with the local culture. Sicily boasts a rich heritage that merges customs from various civilizations, shaping a unique set of social norms and traditions.

When visiting Sicilian towns and interacting with locals, greeting people warmly is appreciated. A simple nod or a smile can go a long way. In more informal settings, a handshake or even two kisses on the cheek (starting with the right) are common among people who are already acquainted. When addressing someone, it's polite to use 'Signor' or 'Signora' followed by their surname until more familiarity is established.

Sicilians place a high value on family and relationships, often prioritizing them above other commitments. This familial respect extends into how they interact with others, including guests and visitors. It's common to be invited into a Sicilian home where hospitality is paramount. If you receive such an invitation, bringing a small gift like pastries, wine, or flowers is a thoughtful gesture. During meals, try to eat everything on your plate as refusing food can sometimes be seen as disrespectful, especially when you're a guest in someone's home.

Dress code in Sicily, like in many parts of Italy, can be quite formal compared to what many travelers might be used to. In cities and when dining out in the evenings, Sicilians tend to dress smartly. When visiting religious sites, modesty is crucial: shoulders and knees should be covered, and hats removed. In conversation, Sicilians are expressive and often use hand gestures to convey their points. While discussing, it's important to be mindful and avoid sensitive topics such as politics and religion unless brought up by your host. Also, be aware that some Sicilians speak in dialects that can differ significantly from standard Italian, which might be challenging to understand.

Another aspect of local etiquette is punctuality. Sicily has a relaxed approach to time, and events or meetings might not start exactly on time. However, as a visitor, you should aim to be punctual as a sign of respect, even if your hosts or local friends are more flexible. Lastly, respecting the environment and public spaces is vital. Sicilians take pride in their surroundings, and littering or disrespecting communal areas is frowned upon. Always aim to leave places as you found them, if not better. By keeping these etiquette tips in mind, you'll not only show respect for Sicilian culture but also enhance your interactions with locals, making your visit more enjoyable and enriching. Sicily's warmth and hospitality are memorable parts of the travel experience, and understanding local customs is key to fully appreciating all that this vibrant island has to offer.

Essential Sicilian Phrases

Learning some essential Sicilian phrases can significantly enrich your visit to Sicily, helping you connect more deeply with locals and enhance your travel experience. While Italian is the official language, Sicilian, a distinct language with its own rich history, is widely spoken across the island. Knowing a few key phrases in Sicilian not only shows respect for the local culture but also opens doors to more authentic interactions.

Firstly, greetings are fundamental in any language, and in Sicilian, a simple "Hello" can be said as "Ciau" (pronounced chow) for both hello and goodbye, similar to the Italian "Ciao." When meeting someone for the first time in the morning, you might want to say "Bon jornu" (Good morning) or use "Bona sira" (Good evening) later in the day.

To express thanks, Sicilians say "Grazzi" (Thank you), and a polite reply would be "Prego" (You're welcome). These basic courtesies can go a long way in showing your appreciation and goodwill.

If you need to ask if someone speaks English, you can say, "Parli ngrisi?" (Do you speak English?). In many tourist areas, locals often speak some English, but they'll appreciate your effort to ask in Sicilian.

In shops or at markets, knowing how to ask the price of something is very useful. Simply say, "Quantu costa?" (How much is this?). When dining out, you might want to know what's recommended, so asking "Chi mi cunsigliati?" (What do you recommend?) can lead to some delightful culinary discoveries.

Should you need directions, a useful phrase is "Unni è?" followed by the place you are looking for, for example, "Unni è il museo?" (Where is the museum?). Responses might involve "Drittu" (straight), "a dritta" (to the right), or "a manca" (to the left), helping you navigate the charming streets of Sicily.

If you are finished with your meal or need to catch someone's attention, saying "Scusassi" (Excuse me) is polite and effective. And when leaving a place, it's courteous to say "A prestu" (See you soon) or "Salutamu" (Goodbye), adding a personal touch to your departure.

By integrating these phrases into your interactions, you'll not only manage everyday situations with greater ease but also demonstrate respect and enthusiasm for Sicilian culture. Locals always appreciate when visitors make an effort to speak their language, even just a few words, which often leads to warmer exchanges and a more immersive experience in the vibrant life of Sicily.

CHAPTER 2

Travel Essentials

Embarking on a journey to Sicily requires some essential preparation to ensure your trip is as smooth and enjoyable as possible. This chapter will provide you with all the necessary information on what to bring, important documents you might need, and tips to keep you safe and healthy while exploring this vibrant island.

Knowing what to pack is crucial, as Sicily's varied landscape and climate mean your suitcase should contain a mix of items for both warm coastal areas and cooler mountain regions. We'll discuss suitable clothing options, gadgets that could enhance your travel experience, and other practical items like adapters for charging your devices. Documents are equally important, especially if you're coming from abroad. We'll cover the types of travel documents you'll need, including visas if applicable, and how to ensure they're all in order before you depart. This includes advice on travel insurance, which can provide peace of mind in case of unexpected events.

Lastly, health and safety are paramount, no matter where you travel. This chapter includes tips on how to stay healthy in Sicily, including what to pack in a travel health kit and how to handle any medical emergencies that might arise. Additionally, we'll touch on the general safety tips that can help you avoid common pitfalls tourists might encounter. By covering these bases, you will be well-prepared to fully immerse yourself in the Sicilian culture, landscapes, and experiences without the stress of last-minute hiccups. This chapter aims to equip you with the knowledge to manage the practical aspects of your trip efficiently, leaving you free to enjoy the rich history and stunning scenery of Sicily.

Visa Requirements

Understanding visa requirements is crucial for anyone planning a trip to Sicily, as it ensures you can enter Italy legally and without any hassle. Since Sicily is part of Italy, the same entry requirements apply as for any other part of the country.

For many travelers, particularly those from within the European Union (EU) or the European Economic Area (EEA), entry into Sicily requires no visa. Citizens from these countries can travel freely to Sicily using their national ID card or passport. This ease of travel allows visitors to focus more on planning their itinerary rather than navigating complicated visa procedures.

Travelers from non-EU/EEA countries, including the United States, Canada, Australia, and New Zealand, usually benefit from the visa exemption policy for stays of up to 90 days within a 180-day period. This means that for short vacations, business trips, or family visits, you do not need a visa if you are a citizen of one of these countries. However, it's important to carry a passport that is valid for at least three months beyond your intended date of departure from the Schengen area, which includes Italy.

For longer stays, or for purposes such as work or study, you will likely need to obtain a visa. There are several types of visas available depending on the purpose of your visit: work visas, student visas, and long-term stay visas are among the most common. Each type of visa has its own requirements and application process, usually involving gathering various documents like proof of financial means, accommodation, and a detailed plan stating the purpose of your stay.

Applying for a visa typically begins at your home country's Italian embassy or consulate. The process can take some time, so it's advisable to apply well in advance of your planned trip. Being prepared with the correct documentation and understanding the timeline for processing can ease the visa application process significantly.

In case your country is not part of the visa exemption scheme, you will need a Schengen visa for short stays. This type of visa allows you to travel within the Schengen area, including Italy, for up to 90 days. It is essential to note that while a Schengen visa allows for travel across the Schengen zone, the primary destination of your visit should be the country that issues you the visa. It is also wise to check the latest information before traveling, as visa policies can change. Keeping up-to-date ensures that you comply with current regulations and avoid any issues upon arrival in Italy. By understanding these visa requirements and preparing accordingly, you can ensure that your visit to Sicily is both enjoyable and compliant with Italian law, allowing you to fully immerse yourself in the rich cultural and historical experiences the island has to offer.

Travel Insurance

Travel insurance is an essential aspect of planning your trip to Sicily, providing peace of mind and protection against unexpected events. Whether you face medical emergencies, lost luggage, or travel disruptions, having a reliable travel insurance policy can significantly reduce the stress and financial impact of such issues.

First and foremost, travel insurance for medical emergencies is crucial. Medical care in Sicily is of high quality, especially in major cities; however, it can be expensive for tourists without proper insurance. A good travel insurance plan will cover medical expenses, ensuring that you receive the necessary treatment without worrying about the cost. This is particularly important in cases of accidents or sudden illness. Some policies also provide coverage for medical evacuation, which means if you need to be transported to a specialized facility or back home for treatment, your insurance will cover these costs. Another key component of travel insurance is coverage for trip cancellations or interruptions. If you need to cancel your trip last minute due to an unforeseen event such as illness, or a family emergency, or if your trip is interrupted due to reasons beyond your control, your insurance policy can reimburse you for non-refundable expenses. This can include pre-paid hotels, flights, and other travel costs that you cannot recover otherwise.

Lost or delayed baggage is another common travel concern that insurance can address. If your luggage is lost, stolen, or delayed, having insurance means you can be compensated for the value of the contents or for the essentials you need to buy while waiting for your luggage. This coverage helps alleviate the inconvenience and cost that comes with baggage issues. Additionally, travel insurance can offer protection against theft and personal liability. If you accidentally cause injury to someone or damage property during your trip, liability coverage can help pay for legal expenses or claims made against you. Similarly, if you fall victim to theft, insurance can provide compensation for stolen money or valuables.

Choosing the right travel insurance policy involves considering the specific risks associated with your travel plans. Look for policies that offer comprehensive coverage that fits the nature of your trip. It's important to read the fine print and understand what is and isn't covered. Some policies may exclude certain activities considered high-risk, like scuba diving or hiking in remote areas, so you might need additional coverage if your travel plans include such activities. Lastly, it's advisable to purchase your travel insurance soon after booking your trip. This way, you're covered if you need to cancel your trip before departing. Many insurance providers also offer 24-hour assistance services, providing support wherever you are in the world, which can be incredibly helpful in navigating unexpected situations while away from home. By securing a suitable travel insurance policy, you safeguard your trip against a range of unexpected events, allowing you to enjoy your Sicilian adventure with greater confidence and security.

Health and Safety Tips

Staying healthy and safe is a crucial part of any travel experience, and Sicily is no exception. As you prepare for your journey to this stunning island, it's important to be aware of basic health guidelines and safety measures to ensure your trip is enjoyable and worry-free. Healthcare in Sicily is accessible and of good quality, especially in larger cities. Tourists should have no major concerns finding hospitals or clinics in case of an emergency.

However, carrying a basic health kit is advisable. This kit should include items such as pain relievers, band-aids, anti-inflammatory drugs, and any prescription medications you might need. Always ensure that your medications are in their original packaging and accompanied by a doctor's note, particularly if they are prescription drugs, to avoid any issues at customs. It's also wise to familiarize yourself with the local emergency numbers. In Sicily, as in all of Italy, you can dial

112 for emergency services. This number can be called from any phone and will connect you to police, medical, and fire services. Regarding food and water, while Sicily's culinary offerings are both safe and delightful, it's important for visitors to take usual precautions. This includes washing hands regularly before eating and ensuring that any street food or seafood dishes are fresh and prepared in hygienic conditions. Sicily's tap water is generally safe to drink, but if you have a sensitive stomach, opting for bottled water might be a better choice.

When it comes to safety, Sicily is relatively secure, but standard travel precautions should be followed. Be mindful of your belongings, especially in crowded areas such as markets, tourist sites, or on public transportation. Petty theft can occur, as in any popular tourist destination, so carrying a money belt or keeping your valuables in a secure place is recommended.

If you're driving, be aware that Sicilian roads can be narrow and winding, especially in rural areas or in the mountains. Local driving styles might also be more aggressive than what you are used to. Always ensure that you have comprehensive insurance if you are renting a car. For those venturing into natural areas, like hiking in the mountains or visiting volcanic sites such as Mount Etna, appropriate preparation is key. This includes having suitable clothing, adequate water, and sun protection. Check the weather forecast before heading out and always inform someone of your plans. Lastly, be cautious of the sun, particularly during the hot summer months. The Sicilian sun can be intense, and it's easy to underestimate its effects.

Regular application of high-SPF sunscreen, wearing a hat, and keeping hydrated are essential practices to prevent sunburn and heatstroke. By adhering to these health and safety tips, you can ensure a safe and fulfilling trip to Sicily. Whether exploring ancient ruins, enjoying local dishes, or simply soaking up the sun at a beautiful beach, keeping these guidelines in mind will help you make the most of your Sicilian adventure without unnecessary setbacks.

CHAPTER 3

Getting There and Around

Navigating your way to and around Sicily is an exciting part of the travel experience, offering various options tailored to different needs and preferences. This chapter is designed to provide you with all the necessary information to make your journey to this beautiful island as smooth as possible and to help you move around comfortably once you arrive.

Getting to Sicily can be done in several ways, depending on where you are coming from. If you're traveling from another country, flying directly into one of Sicily's airports is the most straightforward option. We will explore the different airlines that service Sicily, discuss the major airports, and offer tips on booking flights.

For those who prefer a more scenic route, taking a ferry from mainland Italy is another possibility. Ferries are a fantastic way to see some of the Italian coast before arriving on the island. This chapter will provide details on ferry routes, schedules, and how to get the best deals. Once in Sicily, getting around is an adventure in itself. Whether you choose to rent a car, use public transportation, or even travel by bike, understanding the local transport system is key to enjoying your trip. Car rentals offer flexibility to explore remote areas at your own pace, while buses and trains are a reliable and cost-effective way to travel between major cities and towns.

We will also cover more unique travel options such as the use of scooters, which are popular in Sicilian cities, and give insights into navigating the rural areas where public transport may be less frequent. Additionally, for those planning to hop between the smaller islands off Sicily's coast, information on local boat services will be included. This chapter aims to arm you with all the practical advice needed to choose the best travel options to fit your itinerary in Sicily. With this knowledge, you'll be well-prepared to dive into the heart of Sicilian culture and landscape, making every journey an integral part of your adventure.

Arriving in Sicily: Airports and Entry Points

Arriving in Sicily is an exciting start to your adventure on this historic and picturesque island. Sicily is served by several airports, each acting as a gateway to different parts of the island, making it accessible from nearly any location worldwide.

The main airports in Sicily are Catania-Fontanarossa Airport, Palermo Falcone-Borsellino Airport, and Trapani Birgi Airport. Each of these airports offers various services and has its unique characteristics, catering to the needs of international and domestic travelers. Catania-Fontanarossa Airport is the busiest and the largest airport in Sicily. Located on the east coast, near Catania, it is an ideal entry point for those wishing to explore the eastern parts of the island, including Mount Etna, the baroque cities of Siracusa and Ragusa, and the scenic beaches along the coast. The airport is well-equipped with facilities such as car rentals, public transportation links, and numerous shops and restaurants. Palermo Falcone-Borsellino Airport, situated near Palermo on the north coast, is the second busiest airport. This airport provides easy access to the Sicilian capital, renowned for its rich history, vibrant markets, and beautiful architecture. From here, travelers can also explore the western part of Sicily, including the medieval town of Cefalù and the ancient Greek site of Selinunte. Like Catania, Palermo's airport offers a full range of services, including efficient public transit connections to the city center and other major attractions. Trapani Birgi Airport is smaller and serves as a secondary hub, primarily for low-cost airlines.

It is conveniently located for visiting the westernmost parts of Sicily, including the Egadi Islands, Marsala, and the ancient Greek ruins at Segesta. Although smaller, Trapani airport provides essential services and has public transport and car rental options. For those arriving by sea, there are also several maritime entry points. The ports of Palermo and Catania are the busiest, serving ferry routes from mainland Italy and other Mediterranean destinations. These ports welcome numerous passengers each year and offer services like taxis, buses, and nearby train stations that help travelers continue their journey in Sicily. Upon arrival at any of these airports or ports, you will find clear signs in Italian and English, helping direct you to transportation, luggage claim, and tourist information.

It's advisable to plan your onward journey in advance, whether it involves renting a car, catching a bus, or arranging a transfer, to ensure a smooth continuation of your trip. Sicily's airports and entry points are well-equipped to welcome travelers and provide them with the necessary amenities to start their exploration of this enchanting island. Each airport and port offers unique advantages depending on your travel plans and the areas of Sicily you wish to explore first.

Local Transportation: From Scooters to Buses

Navigating Sicily by local transportation is a practical and immersive way to experience the island's culture and landscapes. From scooters weaving through bustling city streets to buses traversing scenic routes, understanding your options can greatly enhance your travel experience.

Buses in Sicily are a reliable and economical option for getting around. The island has an extensive network of buses that connect major cities like Palermo, Catania, and Messina with smaller towns and rural areas. Buses are particularly useful for reaching destinations that are not served by trains, such as some of the more remote villages and beaches. Tickets can be purchased from tobacco shops, kiosks, or directly from the bus driver, and it is advisable to check the timetable in advance, as frequencies can vary, especially on weekends and public holidays.

Trains offer another convenient way to travel between major towns. Sicily's train network is operated by Trenitalia, with main lines running along the coast. Trains are comfortable and offer stunning views, especially on the route from Messina to Catania and further down to Syracuse. However, the train network is less extensive than the bus system and does not cover the interior parts of the island as comprehensively.

Scooters are a popular mode of transport among locals and tourists alike, offering a flexible way to navigate the often narrow and winding roads, particularly in coastal areas and smaller towns. Renting a scooter can be a thrilling way to explore, giving you the freedom to stop at hidden coves and historical sites at your leisure. When renting a scooter, ensure you have the appropriate license, and always wear a helmet for safety.

Car rentals are another option, providing the greatest flexibility for exploring Sicily at your own pace. Cars can be rented from airports and major towns. While driving gives you access to the island's stunning landscapes and remote areas, be prepared for challenging driving conditions in some parts, especially in the mountainous regions. Also, parking in larger cities can be scarce and often requires payment.

For those staying in cities like Palermo or Catania, public urban transport such as metro and buses is convenient for short distances within the city. Tickets are inexpensive and can be bought at machines and kiosks. Both cities also offer bike-sharing schemes as an eco-friendly way to explore.

Lastly, for visits to the smaller islands off Sicily, such as the Aeolian Islands, ferries and hydrofoils run regularly from ports such as Milazzo and Messina. These sea routes offer not just transportation but also a chance to enjoy some of Sicily's best sea views.

Using local transportation in Sicily not only supports the local economy but also reduces your carbon footprint. Each mode of transport offers a unique perspective of the island, whether you're enjoying the slow pace of a bus journey through the Sicilian countryside or feeling the breeze on a scooter along the coast. With some planning and understanding of the local transport system, you can navigate Sicily efficiently and at your own pace, creating a truly memorable experience.

CHAPTER 4

Accommodation Options

Finding the right place to stay is an essential part of your travel planning, and Sicily offers a wide range of accommodation options to suit any taste and budget. This chapter will explore the variety of choices available, helping you make an informed decision on where to base your Sicilian adventure.

Whether you're looking for a luxurious hotel with sea views, a cozy bed and breakfast tucked away in a picturesque village, or a budget-friendly hostel in the heart of a bustling city, Sicily has something to offer. The island's rich history is reflected in its accommodations, with options ranging from renovated palazzos and monasteries to modern resorts that provide all the comforts of home.

For those interested in immersing themselves in local culture, agriturismos—working farms that offer lodging—are a popular choice. These establishments provide a unique opportunity to experience Sicilian rural life, often with meals prepared from fresh, local ingredients. Another option for an authentic stay are the historic hotels and guest houses located in ancient buildings, where you can sleep within walls steeped in centuries of history.

On the other hand, if independence is a priority, renting a villa or an apartment might be the ideal solution. These accommodations offer the flexibility to create a home-away-from-home, with the freedom to cook meals and come and go as you please. They are particularly suitable for families or groups of friends who require more space and privacy. This chapter will also cover essential tips for booking your accommodation, such as the best times to book for optimal rates, understanding cancellation policies, and considerations for location relative to the attractions you most want to visit. Knowing what each type of accommodation has to offer will help you match your lodging to your travel style and needs, ensuring that your stay in Sicily is as comfortable and enjoyable as possible.

Luxury Resorts

Luxury resorts in Sicily provide an unparalleled experience, blending comfort, elegance, and superior service with the stunning natural beauty and rich cultural heritage of the island. These resorts are not merely accommodations; they offer a complete immersion into luxury, with environments meticulously designed to reflect the artistry and craftsmanship of Sicily.

When staying at a luxury resort in Sicily, guests can expect top-tier accommodations. Rooms are typically spacious and feature high-quality furnishings and décor, often adorned with handcrafted details and artworks unique to Sicilian culture. Many rooms also offer spectacular views—whether it's the serene sea, rugged mountains, or manicured gardens—that guests can enjoy from the comfort of their rooms. The amenities at these resorts cater to every possible need and desire. Dining options are abundant, with multiple restaurants serving gourmet dishes prepared with fresh, locally sourced ingredients. The bold flavors and Mediterranean influences of Sicilian cuisine are highlights, showcasing local seafood, cheeses, and fresh produce in memorable culinary creations. Wellness facilities at these luxury resorts often include full-service spas, which incorporate local products like olive oil, sea salt, and citrus fruits into their treatments, offering a unique local twist to relaxation and rejuvenation. Fitness centers, yoga classes, and private swimming pools are standard features, ensuring guests have ample opportunities for relaxation and activity.

Moreover, the resorts provide personalized concierge services to help guests explore beyond the premises. These services can arrange everything from guided tours of archaeological sites and private boat trips along the coast, to tastings at local wineries, enriching the Sicilian adventure beyond typical tourist paths. Luxury resorts in Sicily also frequently host cultural events and activities, such as cooking classes, wine tastings, and workshops on traditional Sicilian crafts, allowing guests to immerse themselves deeply in local culture.

Here are a few top recommendations for luxury resorts in Sicily, complete with contact information and price ranges:

1. **Verdura Resort**
    - **Address:** SS 115, Km 131, 92019 Sciacca AG, Italy
    - **Phone:** +39 0925 998180
    - **Email:** info.verdura@roccofortehotels.com
    - **Website:** Verdura Resort (https://www.roccofortehotels.com/hotels-and-resorts/verdura-resort/)
    - **Price Range:** $300 to $1,000 per night
    - **Overview:** Set on 230 hectares of olive groves and coastline, the resort is known

for its golf courses, a world-class spa, and organic Sicilian cuisine.

2. Belmond Villa Sant'Andrea
- **Address:** Via Nazionale, 137, 98039 Taormina Mare, Sicily, Italy
- **Phone:** +39 0942 627 1200
- **Email:** reservations.santandrea@belmond.com
- **Website:** Belmond Villa Sant'Andrea (https://www.belmond.com/hotels/europe/italy/taormina/belmond-villa-sant-andrea/)
- **Price Range:** $500 to $1,200 per night
- **Overview:** A refined seaside retreat, this villa offers private beach access, sophisticated dining, and an exclusive atmosphere in the picturesque bay of Mazzarò.

3. Capofaro Locanda & Malvasia
- **Address:** Via Faro, 3, 98050 Salina, Aeolian Islands, Sicily, Italy

- **Phone:** +39 090 984 4330
- **Email:** capofaro@tascaitalia.com
- **Website:** Capofaro Locanda & Malvasia (https://www.capofaro.it/)
- **Price Range:** $250 to $800 per night
- **Overview:** Located on the tranquil island of Salina, Capofaro focuses on the art of hospitality, surrounded by Malvasia vineyards with stunning views of the Mediterranean and the islands of Stromboli and Panarea.

Each of these resorts offers a different slice of Sicilian luxury, catering to various tastes and preferences but all guaranteeing an unforgettable stay. Whether you are looking for a golfing getaway, a romantic retreat, or a cultural immersion, these resorts provide the perfect setting to enjoy Sicily's scenic beauty and historical richness, coupled with impeccable service and exclusive amenities.

Mid-range Hotels

Mid-range hotels in Sicily offer a fantastic balance of comfort, convenience, and cost, making them a preferred choice for a wide array of travelers seeking to explore this vibrant island without breaking the bank.

These hotels cater to those who desire a pleasant stay with essential modern amenities, good service, and access to Sicily's myriad attractions, all at a reasonable price. Mid-range hotels in Sicily typically provide accommodations that focus on comfort and functionality. Guests can expect clean and inviting rooms equipped with comfortable bedding, en-suite bathrooms, air conditioning for the warm Sicilian climate, and often, free Wi-Fi to stay connected. The decor in these hotels usually reflects local design elements, incorporating colors and materials that are characteristic of the Mediterranean landscape, which adds an authentic Sicilian charm to the environment.

The strategic locations of these hotels are particularly advantageous for travelers. Often situated in or near city centers, or conveniently placed in picturesque locales near major tourist spots, mid-range hotels make it easy for guests to explore historical sites, local markets, beautiful beaches, and other cultural attractions. Being centrally located also often provides guests with excellent public transport links, making it straightforward and cost-effective to navigate around the island. Dining options at mid-range hotels generally include an on-site restaurant or dining area, where breakfast is typically served.

Many offer a continental or buffet breakfast with a variety of choices that might include fresh pastries, fruits, cheeses, and cereals, alongside coffee, tea, and juices. Some hotels also provide dinner options that showcase local Sicilian cuisine, known for its robust flavors and fresh ingredients. While these dining facilities might not be as luxurious as those found in high-end resorts, they pride themselves on offering tasty, wholesome food that gives a good introduction to the local fare. Service in mid-range hotels is attentive and geared towards making guests' stays as enjoyable and hassle-free as possible. Staff are usually multilingual and can provide valuable local knowledge about the best places to visit, dining options, and tips on how to get around.

Many hotels also offer additional services like arranging tours, car rentals, and sometimes even airport shuttles. Additionally, mid-range hotels often feature a range of amenities that enhance the comfort of their guests. These may include lounges and bars where guests can relax after a day of sightseeing, garden areas, and sometimes small pools or terraces with views. For families traveling with children, these hotels often offer family rooms that are spacious and may provide cribs or extra beds to accommodate younger guests. In essence, staying at a mid-range hotel in

Sicily allows travelers to enjoy a comfortable and authentic experience that combines convenience with a taste of local culture. These hotels strive to provide a friendly atmosphere where service, comfort, and value meet, making them ideal for travelers who wish to explore Sicily's rich history, indulge in its culinary delights, and soak in the scenic beauty without a hefty price tag. This makes mid-range hotels a smart choice for couples, families, and solo travelers alike, ensuring that everyone can have a memorable and enjoyable stay on this beautiful Mediterranean island.

Here are some recommended mid-range hotels in Sicily, complete with contact details and pricing information:

1. **Hotel Villa Belvedere**
   - **Address:** Via Bagnoli Croci 79, 98039 Taormina, Sicily, Italy
   - **Phone:** +39 0942 23791

- **Email:** info@villabelvedere.it
- **Website:** Hotel Villa Belvedere (https://www.villabelvedere.it)
- **Price Range:** $150 - $300 per night
- **Overview:** Nestled in the charming town of Taormina, Hotel Villa Belvedere offers stunning views of the Ionian Sea and lush gardens. Guests can enjoy a pool area with a panoramic view, a quaint environment, and proximity to the ancient Greek theatre of Taormina.

2. Artemisia Resort

- **Address:** Via Enrico Caruso, 3, 97100 Ragusa, Sicily, Italy
- **Phone:** +39 0932 669119
- **Email:** info@artemisiaresort.it
- **Website:** Artemisia Resort (https://www.artemisiaresort.it)
- **Price Range:** $90 - $180 per night
- **Overview:** This rural hotel, located near Ragusa, is set in a 19th-century farmhouse

renovated to offer modern comforts. The resort features a large garden, an outdoor swimming pool, and a rustic setting that reflects the charm of Sicilian country life.

3. **Algilà Ortigia Charme Hotel**
   - **Address:** Via Vittorio Veneto, 93, 96100 Siracusa, Sicily, Italy
   - **Phone:** +39 0931 465186
   - **Email:** info@algila.it
   - **Website:** Algilà Ortigia Charme Hotel (https://www.algila.it)
   - **Price Range:** $120 - $250 per night
   - **Overview:** Located on the island of Ortigia, the historic center of Syracuse, this hotel is housed in a restored Baroque building. It is ideally situated for exploring the rich history of Syracuse, with easy access to local dining and shopping.

4. **Hotel Porta Felice**

- **Address:** Via Butera, 45, 90133 Palermo, Sicily, Italy
- **Phone:** +39 091 6175678
- **Email:** info@portafelice.it
- **Website:** Hotel Porta Felice (https://www.portafelice.it)
- **Price Range:** $100 - $220 per night
- **Overview:** In the heart of Palermo, this hotel offers modern amenities in a historic setting. Close to the waterfront and Palermo's major cultural attractions, Hotel Porta Felice provides a wellness center, a rooftop terrace, and elegantly furnished rooms.

These mid-range hotels not only assure comfortable lodgings but also serve as excellent bases from which to explore Sicily's diverse attractions. Each offers a unique flavor of Sicilian hospitality and culture, with services designed to enhance your stay on the island.

Budget Stays and Hostels

Budget stays and hostels in Sicily provide an excellent option for travelers who wish to explore this enchanting island without spending a large amount of money on accommodation. These facilities are perfect for students, backpackers, and budget-conscious travelers who value simplicity and social interaction over luxury. Understanding the features and benefits of budget stays and hostels can significantly enhance your travel experience in Sicily.

Hostels in Sicily are not just about offering a place to sleep; they create a community atmosphere that encourages interaction and exchange among guests from around the world. These establishments typically provide shared dormitory-style rooms, although many also offer private rooms for those seeking a bit more privacy. Dorm rooms are usually equipped with bunk beds, and guests share amenities like bathrooms, lounge areas, and kitchens. This setup not only keeps costs low but also facilitates a friendly environment where travelers can meet and share tips and experiences.

In addition to traditional hostels, Sicily offers a variety of other budget accommodations, such as guest houses, budget hotels, and even camping sites, which are great for nature lovers. These options often include basic amenities and services that ensure a comfortable stay without any frills. Guest houses and budget hotels frequently offer private rooms with en-suite bathrooms, and while these are more private than hostels, they still maintain a casual, welcoming atmosphere.

One of the main advantages of staying in hostels and budget accommodations in Sicily is the cost-effectiveness. These places allow you to save money on lodging, which can then be spent on experiencing all that Sicily has to offer, from its rich historical sites and vibrant local markets to its stunning natural landscapes. Moreover, many hostels and budget accommodations are located in central areas or near major transportation links, making it easy to explore the region.

Hostels and budget accommodations often provide a range of communal facilities that enhance the stay experience. Common areas such as kitchens allow guests to prepare their own meals, which is not only budget-friendly but also provides an opportunity to mingle with other travelers. Many places also feature common rooms with books, games, and computers, and some even organize social events like dinners, tours, and outings, which can be perfect for those traveling alone or looking to make new friends.

Additionally, the staff at these accommodations are usually well-versed in local knowledge and can provide invaluable advice on how to get around, what to see, and hidden gems that are off the typical tourist path. They can often suggest affordable local eateries, the best ways to travel, and tips for enjoying Sicily's attractions without overspending.

In essence, budget stays and hostels in Sicily offer more than just a low-cost lodging option; they provide a gateway to experiencing the island's culture in a communal and interactive setting. For many travelers, the memories made in these lively accommodations become as valuable as the sights seen in their travels. Whether you are backpacking across Europe, on a tight travel budget, or simply looking to meet fellow travelers, Sicily's hostels and budget accommodations provide a welcoming and affordable base for exploring this vibrant island.

Here are some recommended budget stays and hostels that provide not only economical accommodation but also a vibrant social atmosphere, perfect for travelers looking to explore Sicily without straining their budgets.

1. **Lol Hostel Siracusa**
   - **Address:** Via Francesco Crispi, 92/94, 96100 Siracusa, Sicily, Italy
   - **Phone:** +39 0931 465088
   - **Email:** info@lolhostel.com
   - **Website:** Lol Hostel Siracusa (http://www.lolhostel.com)
   - **Price Range:** $25 - $60 per night
   - **Overview:** Strategically located near Siracusa's main train and bus station, this hostel offers a range of accommodations from dormitory rooms to private rooms. It features modern amenities, a communal kitchen, a spacious lounge, and is known for its clean, vibrant environment.

2. **Hostel Taormina**
   - **Address:** Via Circonvallazione, 13, 98039 Taormina, Sicily, Italy
   - **Phone:** +39 0942 628782
   - **Email:** booking@hosteltaormina.com
   - **Website:** Hostel Taormina

(https://www.hosteltaormina.com)
- **Price Range:** $30 - $70 per night
- **Overview:** Located in the heart of Taormina, just a few minutes from the historical center, this hostel offers dormitory beds and private rooms with an excellent view of the city. It's a great base for exploring local attractions and enjoys rave reviews for its friendly staff and excellent location.

3. A Casa di Amici Hostel & Guest House
- **Address:** Via Dante Alighieri, 57, 90141 Palermo, Sicily, Italy
- **Phone:** +39 091 765 4652
- **Email:** info@acasadiamici.com
- **Website:** A Casa di Amici Hostel & Guest House (https://www.acasadiamici.com)
- **Price Range:** $20 - $50 per night
- **Overview:** Situated in the vibrant city of Palermo, this hostel offers dorms and

private rooms decorated with artworks and sculptures made by Sicilian artists. It also features musical instruments available for guests, a communal kitchen, and organizes social events, making it a cultural hub as well as a place to stay.

4. Camping La Focetta Sicula
- **Address:** Contrada Siena, 40, 98030 Sant'Alessio Siculo, Messina, Sicily, Italy
- **Phone:** +39 0942 756357
- **Email:** info@lafocettasicula.com
- **Website:** Camping La Focetta Sicula (http://www.lafocettasicula.com)
- **Price Range**: $18 - $40 per night
- **Overview:** For those who enjoy nature, this camping site offers a budget-friendly solution right next to the beach. It provides options for tent camping, caravans, or staying in small bungalows. It's ideal for families and travelers looking for a relaxed and scenic environment.

Unique Accommodations: Agrotourism and Historical Stays

Sicily offers a rich tapestry of unique accommodation options that go beyond traditional hotels, providing visitors with an authentic and immersive experience. Among these, agrotourism and historical stays stand out as particularly enriching choices, each offering a different way to engage with the island's cultural and historical heritage.

Agrotourism, also known as agriturismo, is a form of vacationing in farm-style settings where hospitality is offered by farming families who are keen to share their way of life. This type of accommodation is particularly popular in Sicily, where the agricultural landscape forms an integral part of the region's identity. Agrotourism properties are often situated in picturesque rural areas among olive groves, vineyards, and citrus orchards, providing a tranquil retreat from the busier tourist spots.

Staying at an agriturismo is about more than just enjoying serene surroundings. Guests have the opportunity to experience rural Sicilian life firsthand. Many agrotourism farms offer activities such as cooking classes, where you can learn to make traditional Sicilian dishes using ingredients harvested directly from the farm. Others might include wine tastings, guided nature walks, or even participating in farm activities like picking olives or grapes depending on the season. These experiences not only bring guests closer to nature but also to the food they eat, creating a deeper appreciation and understanding of local culinary traditions.

Historical stays, on the other hand, offer guests the opportunity to live amidst history in meticulously restored properties that have been part of Sicily's architectural landscape for centuries. These accommodations can be found in ancient palazzos, medieval castles, and old monasteries that have been converted into lodgings that offer modern comforts while preserving their historical charm.

These historical properties often retain many of their original features, such as stone walls, wooden beams, and traditional Sicilian tiled floors. Staying in such places is like stepping back in time and offers a tangible connection to the past. Many of these buildings are located in historic centers, allowing easy access to explore Sicily's rich heritage sites. Moreover, the owners of these properties typically are passionate about their history and keen to share stories and insights with their guests, adding an educational element to your stay. Both agrotourism and historical stays in Sicily provide more than just a place to sleep — they offer an experience that can significantly enhance your understanding of the island's culture and history. These accommodations encourage slower, more mindful travel and the chance to engage with the local environment and community in meaningful ways. For travelers seeking a unique and authentic experience, these types of stays are invaluable. They allow you to connect with the land and history in a way that typical hotels cannot offer. Whether it's waking up to a view of vine-covered hills, enjoying a meal made with products from the land around you, or sleeping in a room that has stood for hundreds of years, these experiences contribute profoundly to the memories of your Sicilian adventure.

Here are some recommended places that provide an enriching and authentic Sicilian experience:

Agrotourism Recommendations
1. Zisola Mazzei
- **Address:** Contrada Zisola, 96017 Noto SR, Italy
- **Phone:** +39 0931 835091
- **Email:** zisola@mazzei.it
- **Website:** Zisola Mazzei

(https://www.mazzei.it/en/estates/zisola/)
- **Price Range:** $100 - $250 per night
- **Overview:** Nestled next to the Baroque town of Noto, this elegant estate offers not only accommodation but also a deep dive into the world of Sicilian winemaking. Guests can enjoy wine tours, tastings, and the serene atmosphere of vineyards that stretch out over the rolling hills.

2. **Agriturismo Gigliotto**
    - **Address:** S.S. 117 bis Km 60, 94015 Piazza Armerina, Enna, Italy
    - **Phone:** +39 0935 686066
    - **Email:** info@gigliotto.com
    - **Website:** Agriturismo Gigliotto (https://www.gigliotto.com)
    - **Price Range:** $80 - $150 per night
    - **Overview:** Set in a renovated medieval farmhouse, this agriturismo offers a rustic yet comfortable stay, surrounded by a vast estate of vineyards and olive groves.

Guests can participate in cooking classes, explore the farm, and taste the estate's own produce.

Historical Stays Recommendations
1. Monaci delle Terre Nere
- **Address:** Via Monaci, 95019 Zafferana Etnea CT, Italy
- **Phone:** +39 095 708 3638
- **Email:** info@monacidelleterrenere.it
- **Website:** Monaci delle Terre Nere (https://www.monacidelleterrenere.it)
- **Price Range:** $200 - $600 per night
- **Overview:** Located on the slopes of Mount Etna, this boutique hotel is housed in a historic building amidst a certified organic farm. It beautifully combines luxury with history and offers a unique stay with stunning views of the volcano and the sea.

2. Castello di San Marco Charming Hotel & Spa

- **Address:** Via San Marco, 40, 95011 Calatabiano, Sicily, Italy
- **Phone:** +39 095 641181
- **Email:** info@castellosanmarco.it
- **Website:** Castello di San Marco (https://www.castellosanmarco.it)
- **Price Range:** $150 - $300 per night
- **Overview:** This majestic castle dating back to the 17th century offers a regal experience in a luxurious setting. Located near the sea, it features unique antique furnishings, lush gardens, and a modern spa, providing a perfect blend of history and relaxation.

These unique accommodations not only offer a place to stay but also provide a gateway to experiencing the authentic lifestyle and rich history of Sicily.

CHAPTER 5

Top Attractions

Sicily, an island renowned for its rich tapestry of history, culture, and natural beauty, offers a plethora of attractions that beckon travelers from around the globe. This chapter will guide you through the top attractions that make Sicily a must-visit destination, highlighting the diverse experiences that await every type of traveler.

From the ancient ruins that whisper tales of civilizations past to the vibrant streets that showcase the living culture of today, Sicily holds treasures that span millennia. The island is a spectacle of natural wonders as well, from the fiery craters of Mount Etna to the serene beaches that line its coasts, each offering a unique perspective of Sicily's varied landscapes.

As you journey through Sicily, you will encounter the majestic Valley of the Temples, an archaeological marvel that stands as a testament to Greek art and architecture. Nearby, the Roman mosaics at the Villa Romana del Casale offer a glimpse into the daily lives of ancient Romans through some of the most detailed and vibrant floor mosaics found anywhere in the world.

No visit to Sicily would be complete without exploring its volcanic landscapes. Mount Etna, Europe's largest and most active volcano, provides a dynamic backdrop for hiking and exploration, with guided tours that allow you to safely witness the power of nature's own architecture.

The cultural richness of Sicily continues in its cities, each with their own unique charm. Palermo, the capital, is a tapestry woven with historic markets, Baroque churches, and Norman palaces, telling stories of the myriad cultures that have left their mark on this city. To the east, the hilltop town of Taormina dazzles with its ancient Greek theatre and breathtaking views of the Ionian sea, while the historic island district of Ortigia in Syracuse captures the essence of Sicilian baroque beauty.

This chapter will not only introduce you to these iconic sites but also guide you to hidden gems that enrich your understanding of Sicily's enduring allure. Whether you are drawn to the island for its historical significance, natural beauty, or vibrant local life, Sicily offers a depth of attractions that can transform any visit into an unforgettable journey through time and culture. As we explore these top attractions, prepare to be captivated by the stories and landscapes that make Sicily a timeless treasure in the heart of the Mediterranean.

Historical Landmarks

Sicily, a crossroads of civilizations, offers a rich tapestry of historical landmarks that reflect its diverse cultural heritage. From ancient Greek temples to Norman cathedrals and Arabic palaces, the island is a living museum of millennia of human history, each era leaving behind monuments that tell stories of Sicily's storied past.

One of the most significant historical landmarks in Sicily is the Valley of the Temples in Agrigento, a UNESCO World Heritage site. This archaeological marvel comprises a series of Greek temples built in the 5th century BC. Among them, the Temple of Concordia is one of the best-preserved Doric temples in the world, rivaling those of Athens and Corinth in grandeur and architectural precision. As you walk through this ancient site, you are walking along paths trodden by ancient Greeks, surrounded by the remnants of their grand civilization.

Moving to Sicily's eastern coast, Syracuse was once one of the most significant cities of the ancient Greek world and a fierce rival to Athens. Today, the archaeological park of Neapolis in Syracuse contains a treasure trove of Greek and Roman ruins, including a Greek theatre that is still used for performances, the Roman amphitheater, and the Ear of Dionysius, a limestone cave renowned for its unique acoustics.

In the heart of Palermo, the Palermo Cathedral epitomizes Sicily's complex history. This cathedral has evolved through the ages, with each ruling dynasty adding its own layer of architecture and decoration. Originally designed as a mosque during the Islamic rule in the 9th century, it was later converted into a Norman cathedral and bears elements of Gothic, Baroque, and Neoclassical styles. This architectural palimpsest not only serves as a place of worship but also as a symbol of Sicily's layered history.

Further reflecting the Norman influence on the island is the Monreale Cathedral, located on the slopes overlooking Palermo. This cathedral, built in the 12th century, is famed for its dazzling interiors adorned with golden mosaics depicting scenes from the Old and New Testaments. These mosaics cover more square footage than any other church in the world, except for the Hagia Sophia in Istanbul, showcasing the artistic and cultural heights achieved during Norman rule in Sicily.

Another key historical site is the Castello di Caccamo, one of the largest and best-preserved medieval castles in Sicily. Perched on a rocky mountain, the castle dominates the surrounding countryside, serving as a strategic fortress through the centuries. Touring this castle offers a glimpse into the medieval era of knights and feudal lords, with its imposing halls, massive stone walls, and battlements offering panoramic views of the surrounding landscape.

These landmarks represent just a fraction of the historical wealth Sicily has to offer. Each site not only enriches our understanding of the past but also continues to influence the cultural identity of Sicily today. Exploring these historical sites provides a deeper appreciation of how history is layered in the landscape of Sicily, offering endless lessons and stories that resonate through time.

Natural Wonders

Sicily, a jewel in the Mediterranean, is not only rich in historical and cultural heritage but also abundant in natural wonders that draw visitors from around the world. This island, marked by its dramatic landscapes, offers a diverse range of natural attractions, from active volcanoes and lush mountains to crystal-clear seas and unique geological formations. Exploring these natural sites not only provides a scenic backdrop for outdoor activities but also deepens the appreciation for Sicily's environmental diversity.

Mount Etna, Europe's largest and most active volcano, stands as one of Sicily's most awe-inspiring natural wonders. Dominating the eastern part of the island, Etna is not just a mountain but a living, breathing entity that shapes the life around it. Visitors can take guided tours to safely explore the slopes and craters of this majestic volcano. These tours offer a chance to witness the raw power of nature, observe ancient lava flows, and enjoy panoramic views that stretch across the island to the sea. The fertile volcanic soil also supports a unique ecosystem and allows for the cultivation of vineyards producing distinct wines with robust flavors.

Another remarkable natural feature of Sicily is the Scala dei Turchi, or Turkish Steps, located along the southern coast near Realmonte. This stunning white cliff, made of marlstone, a sedimentary rock with a characteristic white color, naturally carves into a staircase leading down to the Mediterranean Sea. The Scala dei Turchi not only offers breathtaking views against the backdrop of azure waters but also serves as a striking example of natural sculpture, shaped by wind and waves over millennia. In the northeastern region of Sicily, the Nebrodi Mountains stretch across the province, offering lush landscapes and rich biodiversity. This area, part of the larger Nebrodi Park, is an ideal destination for nature lovers interested in hiking, bird watching, and discovering diverse flora and fauna. The park is home to woodlands, lakes, and traditional villages, each offering a glimpse into the rural and wild beauty of Sicily. The Nebrodi Mountains provide a sharp contrast to the volcanic landscapes of Etna, showcasing the ecological variety of the island.

The Alcantara Gorges are another natural spectacle formed by the cooling of ancient lava flows from Mount Etna that have been sculpted by the Alcantara River over thousands of years. These gorges, with their vertical basaltic walls and cold, clear waters, are a popular spot for walking and river trekking. Visitors can walk along paths and steps that lead into the heart of the gorges, where they can swim or simply admire the powerful interplay between the elements that have shaped this unique landscape. Lastly, the salt pans of Trapani and Marsala in western Sicily offer a different yet equally fascinating natural sight. These salt pans have been in use since antiquity, producing sea salt by the natural evaporation of seawater in large shallow pools. The area is not only important for its historical and economic significance but also as a habitat for many species of birds, including flamingos. The salt pans are especially striking at sunset when the setting sun lights up the waters and salt mounds in hues of pink and gold.

These natural wonders of Sicily provide not just scenic beauty but also opportunities for education and recreation. Each site tells a story of geology, ecology, and human interaction with the land, offering visitors a deeper understanding of how Sicily's natural environment has shaped, and been shaped by, the people who live here. Whether you are trekking up the slopes of an active volcano, marveling at a cliff sculpted by the sea, exploring lush mountain paths, navigating river gorges, or watching birds in ancient salt pans, Sicily's natural wonders offer endless possibilities for discovery and delight.

Museums and Galleries

Sicily, with its deep historical roots and rich cultural tapestry, is home to an impressive array of museums and galleries that showcase the island's extensive heritage and artistic achievements. These institutions not only serve as custodians of Sicilian history and art but also provide visitors with insightful narratives about the island's past civilizations, influential art movements, and the daily lives of its people.

One of the most prominent museums in Sicily is the Regional Archaeological Museum Antonio Salinas in Palermo, a treasure trove of ancient artifacts. Named after one of Italy's most notable archaeologists, this museum houses an extensive collection of Greek and Roman antiquities, including intricate mosaics, classical sculptures, and a vast array of decorative arts. The museum's artifacts vividly narrate the stories of the ancient communities that once thrived on the island, making it an essential visit for anyone interested in the archaeological and historical past of Sicily.

In the heart of Syracuse, the Paolo Orsi Regional Archaeological Museum stands out as another significant venue. It is one of the most important archaeological museums in Europe, dedicated to exploring the ancient history of Sicily from the prehistoric to the Greek and Roman periods. The museum's vast exhibits include a remarkable collection of art and artifacts that illuminate the lives of ancient Sicilians, with items ranging from the everyday to the extraordinary. The museum's layout facilitates a chronological journey through Sicily's history, enriched by detailed displays and informational panels that enhance understanding and appreciation of the island's archaeological wealth. For those interested in more contemporary and modern artistic expressions, the Museum of Contemporary Art at the Palazzo Riso in Palermo offers a stark contrast to the ancient relics found in other museums around the island. This museum focuses on contemporary art, featuring works by Sicilian artists as well as international figures. The exhibitions here are often provocative and engaging, reflecting on modern issues through visual arts and helping to bridge the gap between Sicily's rich past and its dynamic present.

Another gem is the Antonino Uccello House-Museum in Palazzolo Acreide, which provides a deeply personal look at Sicilian folk traditions and rural life. This museum is set up to replicate a traditional Sicilian house, offering insights into the daily lives, customs, and crafts of the island's rural inhabitants. The museum is an homage to the folkloristic heritage of Sicily, preserving and presenting the less-documented but equally important aspects of Sicilian culture.

Lastly, the Bellini Museum in Catania is dedicated to Vincenzo Bellini, one of Italy's most renowned opera composers, born in Catania. The museum is located in the house where Bellini was born and features memorabilia, musical scores, and personal belongings of the composer. This museum not only celebrates his musical achievements but also offers insights into the cultural milieu of Sicily during Bellini's lifetime.

Each of these museums and galleries in Sicily plays a crucial role in preserving and interpreting the rich layers of history and culture that define the island. By visiting these cultural institutions, travelers gain a deeper understanding of Sicily's past and present, reflected through artifacts, artworks, and the stories behind them. Whether you are drawn to the ancient relics of bustling Mediterranean empires or the vibrant expressions of contemporary artists, Sicily's museums and galleries offer a comprehensive and enriching experience of this historically pivotal and artistically rich island.

CHAPTER 6

Hidden Gems

Sicily, an island renowned for its majestic volcanoes, ancient ruins, and vibrant cities, also harbors a wealth of lesser-known treasures that await the curious traveler. This chapter delves into the hidden gems of Sicily, those special places off the beaten path that offer a unique glimpse into the island's soul. Exploring these lesser-known spots not only enriches your travel experience but also brings you closer to the true essence of Sicilian life.

Away from the throng of tourists, Sicily hides quaint villages, secluded beaches, and rustic countryside that tell stories not found in typical guidebooks. These places are where you can see Sicilians going about their daily lives, perhaps participating in age-old traditions, crafting local delicacies, or simply enjoying the slow pace of island life. Such experiences provide a deeper understanding and a more personal connection to the island than you could find in its more crowded locales.

You'll discover towns like Caltagirone, famed for its beautiful ceramics and vibrant staircases decorated with intricate tile work. There's also the hilltop town of Erice, where ancient stone streets whisper tales of medieval times, and the tranquil islands of the Egadi archipelago, where the blue of the sea meets the sky in a quiet symphony of nature's beauty. Additionally, this chapter will guide you through hidden natural wonders such as the Alcantara Gorge, carved by ancient volcanic activity, and the quiet coastal reserves where wildlife and flora thrive away from the public eye. You'll learn about small, family-run wineries on the slopes of Mount Etna where you can taste wines made with grapes grown on volcanic soil—an experience distinct from the more commercial vineyards.

Each hidden gem in Sicily offers a story, a taste, or a view that is uniquely its own. By venturing into these less-traveled paths, you will gain more than just photographs; you will collect experiences and memories that resonate with the authentic spirit of Sicily. This chapter aims to equip you with the knowledge to explore these treasures, ensuring that your journey through Sicily is as enriching as it is enchanting.

Off-the-Beaten-Path Destinations

Exploring off-the-beaten-path destinations in Sicily provides a unique opportunity to discover the island's hidden landscapes, untouched nature, and authentic local cultures that are often overshadowed by the more frequented tourist spots. These less-traveled areas offer an in-depth look into the true Sicilian way of life, allowing travelers to experience a deeper connection with the island's traditions and natural beauty.

In the shadow of the well-known Mount Etna lies the Nebrodi Mountains, a serene and lush area that offers stark contrast to the active volcanic landscapes. The Nebrodi Mountains, part of the largest natural park in Sicily, are perfect for those who enjoy outdoor activities like hiking, bird watching, and exploring rich biodiversity. The park encompasses a range of ecosystems, from dense woodlands to high mountain lakes, providing habitats for a variety of wildlife, including the rare Nebrodi black pig, wildcats, and the Bonelli's eagle.

Moving towards the interior of the island, the town of Enna stands as a hidden gem high above the surrounding plains. Known as the 'belvedere' of Sicily due to its panoramic views, Enna offers a glimpse into medieval Sicilian life with its well-preserved castles, ancient churches, and narrow cobblestone streets. The town's elevated position made it historically significant as a strategic lookout point, and today, it provides a quiet retreat from the bustling coastal cities.

On the southwestern coast, away from the typical tourist routes, lies the ancient town of Sciacca. Renowned for its thermal baths that date back to Roman times and its vibrant fishing port, Sciacca is also a center for pottery and ceramic production. Visitors can explore local workshops, enjoy fresh seafood straight from the Mediterranean, and experience the annual carnival, which is one of the liveliest celebrations in Sicily.

Another remarkable destination is the island of Pantelleria, located between Sicily and the North African coast. This volcanic island is famed for its dramatic landscapes, including the unique 'dammusi'—stone dwellings with thick walls and dome roofs designed to collect rainwater. Pantelleria is a haven for those seeking tranquility and rejuvenation, offering thermal springs, mud baths, and a rugged coastline with crystal-clear waters ideal for diving and snorkeling.

For those interested in archaeological sites that are not crowded with tourists, the ancient city of Morgantina in the central region of Sicily presents a fascinating visit. This lesser-known site dates back to the Bronze Age and was an important center during the Hellenistic period. The recent restorations and excavations have revealed stunning finds, including well-preserved statues and intricate mosaics that provide insight into the daily lives of ancient Sicilians.

These off-the-beaten-path destinations in Sicily offer a chance to explore the island's diverse offerings—from mountains and ancient towns to remote islands and archaeological treasures—away from the usual tourist crowds. Venturing into these areas not only enriches your travel experience but also contributes to a sustainable tourism model that benefits small local communities and preserves the natural and historical heritage of Sicily. This deeper exploration encourages a more meaningful connection with the places visited, leaving travelers with a profound appreciation of Sicily's lesser-known yet equally enchanting facets.

Lesser-Known Beaches

Sicily, famed for its cultural richness and volcanic landscapes, is also home to some of the most stunning and lesser-known beaches in the Mediterranean. These secluded spots offer tranquility away from the more popular tourist beaches, providing visitors with a serene escape and the opportunity to experience the island's natural beauty in a more intimate setting.

One such hidden gem is Spiaggia di Marianelli, nestled between Noto and Marzamemi on the southeastern coast of Sicily. This secluded beach is part of the Vendicari Nature Reserve, which serves as a haven for wildlife and a nesting ground for several species of migratory birds. The beach's fine golden sand and crystal-clear waters make it an ideal spot for those seeking peace and natural beauty. With its relative remoteness, Marianelli remains largely untouched by the typical summer crowds, offering a quiet retreat to enjoy the sun and sea.

Further west, near the small town of Realmonte, lies Scala dei Turchi Beach, a lesser-known yet visually striking location. This beach is famous for its stark white marlstone cliffs that resemble a natural staircase descending into the sea. The soft, white rock against the backdrop of turquoise waters creates a breathtaking contrast that is a photographer's dream. While Scala dei Turchi is gaining recognition, it still retains an off-the-beaten-path feel during the quieter months, allowing for a peaceful visit.

In the northwestern part of Sicily, near the town of Castellammare del Golfo, is Cala Bianca. Accessible only by foot or by boat, this small cove offers pristine sandy shores and waters of intense blue. The journey to Cala Bianca involves a scenic hike through rugged coastal terrain, making it a rewarding experience for nature lovers and those looking for a day of adventure and relaxation away from urban noise.

Riserva Naturale dello Zingaro is another spectacular area that boasts several small beaches along its coastline. This nature reserve spans a stretch of unspoiled marine and land ecosystem between Scopello and San Vito Lo Capo. The hiking trails offer stunning views and lead to secluded coves such as Cala Capreria and Cala Berretta, where the clarity of the water and the diversity of marine life make for excellent snorkeling opportunities.

On the island's northern coast, near the town of Cefalù, is Spiaggia delle Salinelle. This extensive, sandy beach is less crowded than its more famous neighbor, Cefalù Beach, and offers ample space for sunbathing and leisure activities. Its length makes it a favorite for long walks and sunset views, with the picturesque backdrop of Sicilian hills adding to its charm.

These lesser-known beaches in Sicily not only provide a retreat from the more crowded tourist spots but also offer a glimpse into the island's varied and stunning coastal beauty. Visiting these beaches allows for a deeper appreciation of Sicily's natural landscapes, offering a quiet refuge and the chance to engage with the island in a more personal and profound way. Each beach, with its unique characteristics and secluded charm, invites visitors to relax, unwind, and enjoy the serene beauty of one of the Mediterranean's most enchanting islands.

Local Markets and Shops

Exploring the local markets and shops in Sicily offers a vivid glimpse into the everyday life and rich cultural tapestry of the island. These vibrant hubs of activity are not just places to purchase goods but are social and cultural gatherings that provide insight into the traditional Sicilian way of life. Each market or shop in Sicily has its own character and specialty, offering everything from fresh produce and artisanal crafts to antiques and designer fashion.

One of the most famous markets in Sicily is La Vucciria in Palermo. This market has existed for centuries and is deeply woven into the fabric of local life. Walking through La Vucciria, you are greeted with a cacophony of sounds, enticing aromas, and the vibrant colors of fresh fruits, vegetables, seafood, and meats. The market comes alive especially at night, turning into a lively spot for tasting street food and enjoying the local ambiance. Here, you can sample traditional

Sicilian street foods like pane con la milza (a spleen sandwich) and arancini (fried rice balls), providing a delicious introduction to Sicilian cuisine.

Another notable market is the Mercato del Capo, also in Palermo, where the influence of Arabic culture on Sicily is evident in the spices, nuts, and fruits on display. The market streets are lined with stalls selling a diverse array of products, from fresh produce and seafood to clothing and household goods. Shoppers and vendors haggle over prices in a scene that has played out daily for generations, showcasing the Mediterranean's bustling market culture.

In Catania, the Pescheria Market offers a special focus on seafood, reflecting the city's close relationship with the sea. Located just behind the Piazza del Duomo, this market is a sensory overload of sights and smells where locals go to get the freshest catch of the day. Surrounding the fish market are stalls featuring vegetables, meats, cheeses, and spices, creating a comprehensive culinary shopping experience.

For those interested in crafts and antiques, the Mercato delle Pulci in Palermo provides a treasure trove of finds. This flea market is the perfect place to hunt for unique items, from vintage Sicilian cart decorations to intricate jewelry and antique furniture. Each stall and item has a story, and part of the fun is learning the history behind these artifacts.

Besides the traditional markets, Sicily also boasts numerous specialty shops that offer unique local products. In towns like Taormina and Cefalù, small boutiques and artisan shops line the ancient streets, selling handmade ceramics, embroidered linens, and fine local wines. These shops are often family-run and provide an opportunity to purchase authentic Sicilian handicrafts that reflect the island's artistic heritage.

Shopping in Sicily's markets and shops provides more than just the opportunity to buy; it offers an immersive experience into the island's culture. It's a chance to interact with local vendors, understand the provenance of the items, and experience the rich tapestry of Sicilian life. Whether you're searching for the freshest ingredients, unique souvenirs, or just a vibrant atmosphere, the markets and shops of Sicily are not to be missed. Through these interactions, visitors gain a deeper appreciation of Sicily as a place of rich history, diverse cultures, and profound human connections.

CHAPTER 7

Things to Do

Sicily, a melting pot of history, culture, and stunning natural landscapes, offers a wide array of activities that cater to every kind of traveler. Whether you're a history enthusiast, nature lover, foodie, or just looking to relax and soak up the sun, Sicily has something special to offer. This chapter will guide you through a diverse selection of activities that will enrich your visit, providing not only enjoyment but also a deeper understanding of what makes Sicily so unique.

Embark on a journey through time as you explore some of the world's best-preserved ancient Greek and Roman sites, such as the Valley of the Temples in Agrigento or the ancient theatre of Taormina, which offers breathtaking views of the Ionian Sea. Discover the rich tapestry of Sicilian

Baroque in cities like Noto and Ragusa, where the architecture tells stories of rebirth and resilience.

For those drawn to natural beauty, Sicily does not disappoint. Hike the rugged trails of Mount Etna, Europe's most active volcano, or find peace on the remote beaches of the Egadi Islands, where the turquoise waters of the Mediterranean provide a perfect setting for relaxation or snorkeling. Birdwatchers and nature enthusiasts will find the saline wetlands of the Stagnone Lagoon near Marsala an excellent spot for observing migratory birds and other wildlife.

Sicilian cuisine, a feast for the senses, offers another layer of experience. Participate in cooking classes where you can learn how to prepare traditional Sicilian dishes, or indulge in wine tasting sessions at local vineyards that take advantage of the island's fertile volcanic soil to produce unique and flavorful wines.

Throughout this chapter, we'll introduce you to the myriad things to do in Sicily, from the bustling street markets of Palermo to the quiet archaeological parks that invite contemplation of the past. Each activity is designed to enhance your visit and provide you with lasting memories of this enchanting island. Whether you're adventuring through its varied landscapes or immersing yourself in the local culture, Sicily offers a profound experience that goes beyond the typical tourist paths.

As a Solo Traveler

Traveling solo in Sicily presents a unique opportunity to immerse oneself fully in the rich tapestry of the island's culture, history, and natural beauty. Solo travel not only fosters independence but also allows for a deeply personal exploration of one of the Mediterranean's most captivating destinations.

For the solo traveler, Sicily offers a safe and welcoming environment to discover at one's own pace. The island's well-trodden tourist paths and less explored routes alike provide ample opportunity for adventure and discovery. One of the first aspects solo travelers will appreciate is the warmth and hospitality of the Sicilian people. Locals often take pride in sharing their knowledge and passion for their homeland, making a solo traveler feel right at home.

Navigating Sicily can be an enriching experience, with reliable public transportation linking major cities and towns. The extensive network of buses and trains makes it easy to move from one place to another, exploring diverse landscapes and cultural sites. Renting a car might offer more flexibility and the chance to venture into more secluded areas, which can be especially rewarding in Sicily's countryside, where ancient ruins and traditional villages abound.

Safety, a crucial consideration for any solo traveler, is well-regarded in Sicily. Common sense precautions are advisable, such as guarding personal belongings and staying aware of your surroundings, especially at night. However, the general atmosphere in Sicilian towns and cities is welcoming and secure.

Solo travelers can enrich their journey by engaging in local activities that might not be as accessible when traveling in groups. Participating in a cooking class, for instance, can offer more than just culinary skills; it's a chance to engage with locals and learn about Sicilian lifestyle and cuisine directly from its source. Similarly, guided tours, especially those focused on specific interests such as wine-making, history, or hiking, can provide insights and connections that enhance the travel experience.

The island's myriad cultural offerings—from the puppet theaters of Palermo to the ancient Greek theatres of Syracuse and Taormina—offer profound solo experiences where one can enjoy the artistic heritage of Sicily at a personal pace. Additionally, the natural reserves, such as the Zingaro Nature Reserve and the beaches of Lampedusa, provide peaceful retreats to appreciate nature's beauty solo.

Solo dining in Sicily is also a delight, with countless cafes, trattorias, and street food vendors offering a taste of Sicilian gastronomy in a casual and inviting atmosphere. Sitting at a street cafe with a glass of local wine or enjoying a gelato while walking through a bustling market can be as rewarding as a full-course meal in a fancy restaurant.

Finally, accommodations in Sicily cater well to solo travelers. From cozy bed-and-breakfast establishments in historic buildings to hostels where other solo travelers gather, there are options to suit any preference and budget. These accommodations often serve as additional venues to meet people, exchange stories, and gather tips for further travels around the island.

Traveling alone in Sicily allows for an unparalleled degree of freedom to explore, reflect, and grow. Each experience, whether it's marveling at a sunset over the salt pans of Trapani or finding an unexpected historical gem in a remote mountain town, becomes a personal chapter in the larger story of your Sicilian adventure.

For Couples: Romantic Escapes

Sicily, with its enchanting landscapes, rich history, and captivating culture, offers an idyllic setting for couples seeking a romantic escape. The island's natural beauty, combined with its serene villages and vibrant cities, creates a perfect backdrop for love and adventure. Here, romance is not just found in its sunsets or scenic views, but in every aspect of Sicilian life, from its food to its architecture and beyond.

For couples looking to immerse themselves in the romantic atmosphere, the historic town of Taormina is a must-visit. Perched on a cliff overlooking the Ionian Sea, Taormina boasts breathtaking panoramas that have enamored visitors for centuries. Couples can stroll along its medieval streets, visit the ancient Greek theatre, and dine in restaurants offering spectacular views of Mount Etna and the azure waters below. The town's intimate setting is ideal for those who wish to lose themselves in beauty and history.

Another exquisite locale for romantic exploration is the Aeolian Islands, a UNESCO World Heritage site just off the northeastern coast of Sicily. These islands are famed for their rugged volcanic beauty, therapeutic hot springs, and crystal-clear waters. Couples can enjoy leisurely boat trips around the islands, relax in secluded coves, or watch stunning sunsets from the terraces of charming boutique hotels. The slow pace of life here is perfect for couples seeking to unwind and connect with each other.

Couples interested in gastronomy and Sicilian wines will find the countryside around Mount Etna an enchanting destination. The fertile volcanic soils of the region produce some of Italy's most distinct wines. Visiting local vineyards can provide an intimate glimpse into the winemaking process, complete with tastings and meals that showcase local specialties. These experiences offer a delightful way to spend time together while engaging the senses.

For those who revel in the pleasures of secluded beaches, the southern coast of Sicily hides several gems where couples can enjoy the sun and sea in privacy. Places like the Scala dei Turchi, with its white marl cliffs, or the remote beaches near the Turkish Steps offer couples a tranquil setting to bask in each other's company against a backdrop of stunning natural beauty.

Couples with a penchant for history and culture will find the city of Syracuse an irresistible draw. The city's rich history, evidenced by its ancient ruins, baroque churches, and the charming island of Ortigia, provides countless opportunities for discovery. Romantic walks along the historic streets, sunset cruises around the harbor, and evenings spent in atmospheric restaurants make Syracuse a memorable stop for lovebirds.

In these settings, Sicily offers more than just typical romantic activities; it provides a deep connection to a place where every corner, every stone, and every wave tells a story. For couples, it's these shared experiences, these moments of discovering something eternal together, that turn a simple vacation into a profound romantic journey. Sicily, with its endless capacity to enchant and inspire, stands as a timeless destination for lovers seeking both relaxation and adventure in a land rich with passion and beauty.

With Kids: Family-Friendly Activities

Sicily, with its vibrant culture, rich history, and diverse landscapes, offers a plethora of activities that cater to families traveling with children. The island's natural wonders, historic sites, and child-friendly attractions provide an ideal setting for a family vacation that is both educational and fun.

One of the highlights for families visiting Sicily is the opportunity to explore its active volcanoes. Mount Etna, Europe's largest active volcano, offers various guided tours that are both safe and educational. Families can take a cable car ride up the mountain, followed by a jeep tour that brings them close to the summit craters. The experience of walking on ancient lava flows and seeing steam vents up close can captivate children and adults alike, offering a firsthand lesson in geology and the natural forces that shape our planet.

Beaches in Sicily are another great attraction for families. The island boasts numerous sandy beaches with shallow waters perfect for young swimmers. Mondello, near Palermo, is particularly popular among families due to its white sandy beach and amenities like playgrounds and snack bars. On the eastern coast, the beaches of Taormina provide breathtaking views and crystal-clear waters, along with facilities that ensure a comfortable day out for families.

For a day filled with adventure and learning, the Madonie Adventure Park offers obstacle courses set in a beautiful forested area within the Madonie Regional Natural Park. It's designed for different age groups, ensuring that everyone from toddlers to teens can enjoy activities suited to their level of adventure, including zip lines, bridges, and climbing nets. This park not only stimulates physical activity but also encourages problem-solving and confidence-building among kids.

Sicily is also rich in history, and many of its archaeological sites are surprisingly kid-friendly. The Valley of the Temples in Agrigento, for example, is an open-air museum where children can marvel at the remains of ancient Greek temples. Interactive guides and storytelling tours are available to make the history come alive for young visitors. Similarly, the ancient theatre of Syracuse offers a captivating view into the past, where families can sit in the same seats once occupied by ancient Greeks and Romans.

Apart from the physical sites, several museums in Sicily offer workshops and activities specifically designed for children. The Puppet Museum in Palermo, for instance, not only displays a fascinating collection of traditional Sicilian puppets but also hosts puppet-making workshops and puppetry shows that can engage children in the art and storytelling traditions of the island.

In Catania, the Museo Civico di Castello Ursino hosts family-friendly exhibits where children can interact with displays that explain the city's history through engaging multimedia presentations. This museum is housed in an impressive castle, adding a sense of adventure to the educational experience.

These activities in Sicily offer children the opportunity to learn through exploration and play, making their vacation both memorable and enriching. From the heights of Mount Etna to the depths of the Mediterranean at the beaches, and through the time-traveling experiences at historical sites and museums, Sicily provides a diverse playground for families to explore, learn, and bond together.

As a Family: Group Adventures

Sicily, a captivating Mediterranean island, is a treasure trove of adventures that are perfect for families seeking to create lasting memories together. This diverse island offers a plethora of activities that cater to all ages, making it an ideal destination for family vacations where education, culture, and fun blend seamlessly into the backdrop of an ancient and dynamic landscape.

Exploring Sicily as a family provides a unique opportunity to engage in activities that are as informative as they are exhilarating. One of the key attractions for families is the chance to explore Sicily's diverse natural environments. The island's geography ranges from the fiery craters of Mount Etna to the serene beaches of its extensive coastline and the lush trails of its nature reserves. For example, a guided tour of Mount Etna can be an educational highlight, offering lessons in geology and natural history as families witness an active volcano up close. These tours are tailored to be safe for children and engaging for adults, ensuring that every family member gains from the experience.

The beaches of Sicily are particularly appealing for families. The gentle waters of the Mediterranean are ideal for swimming and snorkeling, where both kids and adults can explore marine life in clear blue waters. Beaches like Isola Bella in Taormina not only provide stunning scenery but also opportunities for eco-friendly water sports, such as kayaking and paddleboarding, that families can enjoy together.

For those interested in history and culture, Sicily abounds with archaeological sites and museums that are accessible to visitors of all ages. Places such as the Valley of the Temples in Agrigento offer a glimpse into ancient civilizations with well-preserved temples and an engaging archaeological museum where interactive exhibits capture the imaginations of younger visitors.

Similarly, the historic cities of Palermo and Catania offer cultural experiences that include puppet theatres, which preserve and share the traditional art form of puppetry with engaging performances that fascinate children and adults alike.

Adventure also awaits in the natural reserves such as the Madonie or Nebrodi parks, where families can hike well-marked trails and discover the native flora and fauna of Sicily. These parks often offer educational workshops and guided nature walks that help children learn about the environment and the importance of conservation while enjoying the great outdoors.

Furthermore, Sicily's culinary offerings provide another layer of exploration. Families can visit local markets and farms where they can learn about Sicilian cuisine and participate in cooking classes tailored for all ages. These hands-on experiences are not only fun but also educational, as they teach kids about local ingredients and culinary techniques in a family-friendly setting.

Each of these activities in Sicily is designed to strengthen family bonds through shared experiences that are enriching and fun. From the adrenaline of exploring a live volcano to the tranquility of a coastal hike, and the joy of discovering ancient myths through interactive storytelling or puppet shows, Sicily offers a broad range of group adventures that can be tailored to family needs. These experiences allow families to learn together, challenge each other, and most importantly, enjoy every moment of their adventure in one of the most vibrant and culturally rich islands of the Mediterranean.

As a Senior Traveler

Traveling to Sicily as a senior traveler offers a wealth of opportunities to enjoy leisure, cultural immersion, and relaxation in a setting that combines the allure of rich history with the beauty of the Mediterranean landscape. Sicily is an ideal destination for senior travelers, offering a comfortable climate, accessible attractions, and a range of activities tailored to those who might favor a more relaxed and enriching travel experience.

For senior visitors, Sicily's historical sites provide a fascinating glimpse into the past without requiring strenuous physical effort. Many of these sites are well-equipped with amenities to ensure accessibility, including clear signage, ramps, and occasionally, transportation services like small electric cars or shuttle buses. For instance, the Valley of the Temples in Agrigento, one of Sicily's most famous archaeological sites, offers paved paths and guided tours on eco-friendly vehicles, making it easy for seniors to explore this vast area comfortably.

In cities like Palermo and Catania, guided tours specifically designed for seniors can help make the most of visiting historical landmarks, museums, and churches. These tours often take a slower pace, with plenty of stops for rest, making them ideal for those who prefer to take their time. Walking through the vibrant markets and quaint streets of these cities not only provides light exercise but also a chance to engage with local Sicilian culture firsthand.

Sicily is also renowned for its thermal spas, which can be particularly appealing to senior travelers looking for therapeutic experiences. The spas of Sciacca and Termini Imerese are celebrated for their mineral-rich waters, which are said to have healing properties that help with various ailments such as arthritis and rheumatism. Spending a day at one of these spas can be a soothing, rejuvenating experience, offering health benefits alongside relaxation.

The island's natural beauty is easily accessible through scenic drives along the coast or into the heart of Sicily's countryside, where one can explore charming villages and sample local cuisine. Many of these villages, like Erice and Cefalù, offer gentle walking routes and plenty of cafés and benches where one can sit back and enjoy the surroundings at a leisurely pace.

Additionally, Sicily's culinary offerings are a delight for any palate, with options ranging from upscale restaurants to local trattorias that offer traditional Sicilian meals. Dining in Sicily is not just about the food—it's about the experience of enjoying long, leisurely meals with good wine, often accompanied by breathtaking views or in historic buildings that resonate with character.

Cultural events such as opera performances at the ancient theatre of Taormina or live folk music evenings provide enriching entertainment that doesn't require physical exertion. Many of these events are held in spectacular settings, combining cultural enrichment with the chance to enjoy Sicily's lovely evening ambiance.

Traveling in Sicily for seniors is not only about comfort and accessibility but also about experiencing a deep connection with the island's culture, history, and natural beauty. Each activity, visit, and meal is an opportunity to explore and enjoy at a pace that respects the needs and preferences of the senior traveler, ensuring a trip that is as full and satisfying as it is comfortable and accessible.

Outdoor Activities: Hiking, Sailing, and More

Sicily, a treasure trove of natural landscapes ranging from rugged mountains to sparkling seas, offers a diverse array of outdoor activities that cater to adventure enthusiasts of all kinds. Whether you're a hiker seeking scenic trails, a sailor yearning for the open waters, or someone who enjoys leisurely outdoor pursuits, Sicily provides ample opportunities to engage with nature in exciting and fulfilling ways.

Hiking in Sicily is a particularly rewarding experience, thanks to the island's varied terrain and breathtaking vistas. The island is home to several notable hiking trails that cater to all levels of experience. One of the most famous is the ascent of Mount Etna, Europe's tallest and most active volcano. The trails leading up to Etna's summit offer not only the thrill of hiking an active volcano but also the chance to witness unique geological formations and a panoramic view of the island that stretches out to the sea.

Another exceptional hiking area is the Madonie Regional Natural Park. Located in the northern part of Sicily, this park features some of the most beautiful and diverse landscapes on the island. Hikers can explore well-marked trails that meander through lush forests, rocky outcrops, and past ancient hilltop villages. The park is also a haven for wildlife enthusiasts, as it is home to an array of species that are endemic to Sicily.

Sailing around Sicily offers a different perspective of the island's stunning coastline and provides access to lesser-known areas that are often inaccessible by land. The Tyrrhenian, Mediterranean, and Ionian seas that surround Sicily are dotted with picturesque islands, secluded coves, and vibrant marinas that make sailing here a delightful experience. Whether you choose to charter a yacht for a day or join a guided sailing tour, the waters of Sicily offer tranquil sailing conditions and the chance to indulge in water sports such as snorkeling and diving in some of the clearest waters in the Mediterranean.

In addition to hiking and sailing, Sicily's diverse landscape is well-suited for cycling, bird watching, and even paragliding. Cycling tours, especially in the areas around the Val di Noto, provide a leisurely way to explore the countryside, with routes that offer a mixture of coastal and inland scenery punctuated by baroque towns and historic sites. For bird watchers, the salt pans near Trapani and the Vendicari nature reserve are excellent spots to observe migratory birds in their natural habitat.

For those seeking a rush of adrenaline, paragliding over the Sicilian landscape offers an unforgettable experience. The town of Tusa, located on the northern coast, is a popular spot for paragliding, where one can glide over the rugged coastline and turquoise waters, enjoying views that are as majestic as they are thrilling.

Engaging in outdoor activities in Sicily is not just about physical exercise; it's about connecting with the natural world in a meaningful way. Each activity offers a chance to appreciate the unique beauty of Sicily, from its highest peaks to its deepest blue seas, and provides a deeper understanding of why this island has captivated the hearts of travelers for centuries. Whether you are hiking ancient trails, sailing through the Aeolian Islands, or cycling past olive groves, Sicily's landscapes provide the perfect backdrop for an outdoor adventure.

CHAPTER 8

Dining and Nightlife

Sicily, a Mediterranean culinary paradise, offers a vibrant tapestry of tastes and nocturnal delights that await every traveler. This chapter delves into the diverse and rich dining and nightlife experiences that embody the essence of Sicilian culture. Whether you're seeking to savor authentic Sicilian dishes, sip on local wines, or dance the night away, Sicily provides an enchanting backdrop that combines traditional charm with modern vivacity.

Sicilian cuisine, a feast for the senses, is deeply rooted in the island's history and geographical bounty. From the freshest seafood caught in the Mediterranean waters to the lush produce harvested from the fertile volcanic soil of Mount Etna, the ingredients here are as natural as they are flavorful. Dining in Sicily might start with delectable antipasti plates followed by rich pastas, grilled meats, or succulent fish, each dish telling a story of the island's Greek, Arabic, and Norman influences. Not to forget the sweet delights such as cannoli and cassata, which offer a perfect ending to any meal.

Equally compelling is Sicily's nightlife, which ranges from laid-back evenings in quaint wine bars to lively festivals in ancient squares. Each locale offers a different flavor of Sicilian life. In the larger cities like Palermo and Catania, you can find a variety of options from opera performances and live music venues to buzzing nightclubs and bars. The smaller towns, with their charming piazzas and seaside promenades, offer a more subdued but equally enjoyable atmosphere where you can enjoy a glass of local wine or a late-night gelato under the stars.

This chapter will guide you through Sicily's best eateries, from rustic trattorias to high-end restaurants, and detail the vibrant nightlife options available. You'll learn not only about the traditional foods and innovative dishes to try but also about the unique settings in which to enjoy them—be it a beachfront café, a rooftop bar overlooking the twinkling lights of a bustling city, or a historic palazzo turned into a modern gastropub.

Immersing yourself in the dining and nightlife of Sicily offers more than just meals and entertainment—it is an exploration of a lifestyle that celebrates the joy of sharing good food and good times. It's an experience that promises to captivate your palate and create memories that linger far beyond the last bite or the final note of the evening's serenade.

Traditional Sicilian Cuisine

Traditional Sicilian cuisine is a delightful exploration of flavors and history, reflecting the island's complex cultural tapestry woven through centuries of conquest and trade. The food in Sicily is characterized by its diversity, quality of ingredients, and the profound flavors that capture the essence of the Mediterranean diet. This culinary richness provides not only a feast for the palate but also an insightful window into the island's cultural heritage.

Sicilian cooking is deeply rooted in the island's agricultural bounty. The fertile volcanic soil of the region yields exquisite fruits, vegetables, and grains, while the surrounding seas offer an abundant supply of fresh seafood. These resources form the foundation of a diet where simplicity meets richness, and every meal tells a story of the land and sea.

One of the cornerstones of Sicilian cuisine is its seafood, which is prepared with minimal embellishment to highlight its freshness. Dishes such as 'Sarde a Beccafico', a traditional recipe involving fresh sardines stuffed with breadcrumbs, raisins, pine nuts, and herbs, showcase the creative use of local ingredients. Another favorite is 'Spaghetti ai Ricci', pasta served with sea urchin, an ingredient that epitomizes the taste of the Sicilian sea.

Sicily is also renowned for its street food, which offers an accessible taste of its culinary heritage. Arancini, fried rice balls filled with ragù, mozzarella, and peas, are a perfect example of Sicilian ingenuity in creating hearty, delicious food suitable for on-the-go eating. Panelle, chickpea fritters, are another popular snack that is both simple and profoundly satisfying.

The island's desserts are equally notable, often featuring locally produced ricotta cheese, almonds, and citrus fruits. Cannoli, crispy pastry shells filled with sweet, creamy ricotta, are perhaps the most iconic Sicilian dessert. Equally beloved are 'Cassata Siciliana', a rich cake adorned with candied fruits and marzipan, and the less globally known but equally delicious 'Cuccidati', fig-stuffed cookies that are traditionally enjoyed during festive seasons.

Sicilian cuisine also features a variety of cheeses and wines that complement its meals. Cheeses like 'Pecorino Siciliano', made from sheep's milk, and 'Caciocavallo', a cow's milk cheese, are often enjoyed with regional wines, including the robust Nero d'Avola or the sweet Marsala. These pairings are crucial to the Sicilian dining experience, reflecting the island's pasture and vineyard wealth.

The cooking methods and recipes of Sicily carry influences from the various cultures that have inhabited the island, including Greek, Arab, and

Norman. This fusion is evident in the use of ingredients like saffron, raisins, and nuts in savory dishes, which give Sicilian cuisine its distinctive flavors and aromas.

In Sicily, food is more than just sustenance; it is a celebration of life and a proud expression of the island's history and culture. For anyone visiting, indulging in the traditional cuisine provides not only a taste of genuine Sicilian hospitality but also an understanding of the island's rich cultural heritage, making every meal a memorable educational journey.

Best Restaurants for Every Budget

Sicily offers a diverse dining landscape that caters to all tastes and budgets, providing both locals and tourists with an array of gastronomic experiences. From Michelin-starred restaurants to family-run trattorias and street food stalls, the island's culinary offerings reflect its rich cultural heritage and agricultural bounty. This detailed guide explores some of the best dining options across Sicily, ensuring every traveler can enjoy the flavors of the island, regardless of budget.

Michelin-Starred Dining

For those looking to indulge in high-end dining, Sicily boasts several Michelin-starred restaurants that offer innovative dishes inspired by traditional Sicilian ingredients. One standout is La Madia in Licata, where Chef Pino Cuttaia uses local seafood and fresh produce to create artful interpretations of classic flavors. Another acclaimed restaurant is Duomo in Ragusa Ibla, which features a menu that combines Sicilian culinary traditions with modern techniques, all served in a sophisticated setting.

Mid-Range Options

Mid-range restaurants in Sicily often provide the best balance between quality and cost, offering authentic Sicilian dishes made with local ingredients. Trattoria Da Nino in Taormina is a perfect example. It offers spectacular views of the Mediterranean and a menu that features fresh seafood and homemade pasta. Another excellent choice is Osteria dei Vespri in Palermo, where the focus is on reviving old Sicilian recipes with a contemporary twist, ensuring a delightful dining experience that reflects the island's gastronomic heritage.

Budget-Friendly Eats

For travelers on a tight budget, Sicily's numerous trattorias and street food options provide delicious meals without a hefty price tag. In Palermo, Antica Focacceria San Francesco serves traditional Sicilian street food, including panelle (chickpea fritters) and arancini (stuffed rice balls), in a historic setting. Similarly, Taverna Azzurra in Syracuse offers simple, flavorful dishes such as pasta with fresh sardines and wild fennel, allowing diners to enjoy hearty meals at affordable prices.

Specialty Food Shops

In addition to restaurants, Sicily's specialty food shops are great for sampling local products without committing to a full meal. Fratelli Burgio in Siracusa, for instance, offers a range of Sicilian cheeses, cured meats, and other delicacies that reflect the island's agricultural richness. These shops often provide tastings and sell products that make excellent snacks or souvenirs.

Outdoor and Seasonal Markets

Visiting local markets is another economical way to taste Sicilian cuisine. Markets such as Mercato del Capo in Palermo are bustling with vendors selling everything from fresh produce and seafood to ready-to-eat treats. These markets not only offer a glimpse into the daily life of Sicilians but also provide fresh, budget-friendly food options that are perfect for a casual meal.

This overview of dining options in Sicily for every budget underscores the island's culinary diversity and its capacity to cater to every type of diner. Whether you are splurging on a meal at a top-tier restaurant or grabbing a quick bite at a street stall, Sicily's food scene is sure to enrich your travel experience, leaving you with lasting memories of the island's flavors and culinary traditions.

Nightlife: Bars and Live Music Venues

Sicily's nightlife offers a vibrant tapestry of experiences that cater to a wide array of tastes, ranging from quaint bars with traditional live music to modern venues that feature international DJs and bands. This diverse scene provides not only entertainment but also a glimpse into the cultural fabric of the island, where the warmth of its people and the richness of its traditions create unforgettable evenings.

Bars and Pubs

Bars and pubs in Sicily often embody the island's relaxed lifestyle and are great places to mingle with locals. In Palermo, the Vucciria Market transforms at night into a bustling hub where bars serve local wines and cocktails alongside street food. Similarly, Cantina Siciliana in Trapani offers a rustic setting with a selection of Sicilian wines and appetizers, making it a favorite for those who enjoy a laid-back atmosphere with a touch of local flavor.

Another notable spot is Bar Turrisi in Castelmola, which is famous not only for its unique decor but also for its almond wine. This bar provides a unique Sicilian experience with its balconies offering stunning views of Mount Etna and the Ionian coast, making it an ideal spot for a romantic night out or a relaxed drink with friends.

Live Music Venues

For live music enthusiasts, Sicily boasts several venues that host a range of performances from traditional Sicilian folk music to contemporary international acts. In Catania, MA (Musical Association) offers an eclectic program of live music ranging from jazz to rock and electronica, housed in a space that also serves as a cultural center for the arts.

In the summer months, the ancient Greek theatres of Siracusa and Taormina become venues for international music and arts festivals. Watching a live performance in these historic settings is a magical experience; the ancient stones and open skies add a timeless element to the concerts, making these events a must-do for visitors.

Clubs and Dance Venues

For those seeking a more energetic nightlife scene, Sicily's clubs and dance venues offer vibrant nightlife options. Banacher in Aci Castello near Catania is one of Sicily's most famous discotheques. With its large outdoor pool and garden, it attracts top Italian and international DJs, offering a stylish party atmosphere.

Cultural Nights

Many bars and venues in Sicily also host cultural nights that include wine tastings, literary readings, and live painting sessions. These events are perfect for those who look to combine nightlife with cultural enrichment. Teatro dei Pupi (Puppet Theatre) in Palermo offers evening shows that revive the traditional Sicilian puppetry arts, providing an engaging and culturally rich nightlife activity.

The nightlife in Sicily encapsulates the island's spirit of hospitality and celebration. Whether you are toasting with a glass of Nero d'Avola in a cozy bar, enjoying a live folk band in a bustling piazza, or dancing beneath the stars at a beachfront club, the island offers myriad ways to enjoy its nocturnal charms. Each venue not only entertains but also deepens the visitor's appreciation of Sicily's diverse cultural landscape, making each night out an enriching experience.

CHAPTER 9

Cultural Experiences

Sicily, a crossroads of Mediterranean civilizations, offers a rich palette of cultural experiences that engage the senses and enrich the mind. This chapter delves into the myriad cultural activities available to tourists, each offering a unique perspective on Sicily's layered history and vibrant contemporary life. From ancient Greek theaters to lively modern-day festivals, Sicily provides a continuous dialogue between the past and present, making it an ideal destination for those who seek to immerse themselves in deep cultural understanding.

In this exploration, we will guide you through Sicily's most compelling cultural offerings. You will learn about the traditional puppet theaters of Palermo, where intricate marionettes enact classic folk stories and historical dramas, preserving a form of storytelling that has been designated a UNESCO Masterpiece of the Oral and Intangible Heritage of Humanity. These performances offer a fascinating glimpse into Sicilian folklore and are a testament to the island's rich oral traditions.

We will also introduce you to the vibrant festivals that mark Sicilian life, where religious and secular celebrations fuse in a kaleidoscope of color, music, and ritual. You'll experience the famed Holy Week processions, where towns like Trapani and Caltanissetta turn into stages for ancient rites. Similarly, summer brings a plethora of festivals celebrating everything from art and music to food and wine, highlighting Sicily's generous and celebratory spirit.

Art lovers will revel in the wealth of museums and galleries that dot the island, showcasing both classical and contemporary art. Sicily's archaeological museums, in particular, offer an unparalleled look at ancient artifacts recovered from numerous sites across the island, telling stories of Sicily's Greek, Roman, and Norman periods through preserved art and everyday objects.

Additionally, we'll take you through the traditional markets that are a daily feature in Sicilian towns and cities. These markets aren't just places to buy food; they are cultural arenas where one can experience the hustle and bustle of Sicilian life, engage with local vendors, and taste the fresh produce that forms the basis of Sicilian cuisine.

By the end of this chapter, you'll have a deeper appreciation of how Sicily's cultural fabric is woven from threads of its complex history, passionate people, and dynamic traditions. Each cultural experience in Sicily is more than just an activity; it's an opportunity to connect with the soul of the island, offering insights and memories that go far beyond the conventional tourist path.

Festivals and Events

Sicily, with its rich tapestry of history and culture, is renowned for its vibrant festivals and events that celebrate a wide array of customs, religious traditions, and the arts. These gatherings are not only a spectacle of colors and sounds but also a profound expression of the island's identity and heritage, offering visitors an invaluable opportunity to engage deeply with the local community and its traditions.

One of the most iconic celebrations in Sicily is the Festa di Santa Rosalia in Palermo, known locally as the "Festino," which is the largest festival in the city and one of the most important in Sicily. Held annually in July, this festival celebrates the patron saint of Palermo with a huge procession that winds through the streets, featuring elaborate floats, traditional music, and hundreds of participants dressed in historical costumes. The Festino culminates in a spectacular fireworks display that lights up the night sky, symbolizing the triumph of Saint Rosalia over the plague in the 17th century.

Another significant event is the Infiorata di Noto, a flower festival that takes place every May in the baroque town of Noto. This event features incredible floral displays, with artists creating detailed and elaborate designs along the streets using petals, seeds, and other natural materials. The vibrant patterns and the sweet fragrance of fresh flowers transform the town into an open-air gallery, celebrating the beauty of spring and the skill of its artists.

In the small hilltop town of Sutera, the Living Nativity transforms the entire town into a reenactment of Bethlehem during the Christmas season. Residents and actors participate in portraying life as it was two thousand years ago, with craftspeople working in ancient workshops, shepherds tending to their flocks, and traditional music filling the air. This event provides a unique way to experience the Christmas story and is a profound community effort to preserve and share their heritage.

The Almond Blossom Festival of Agrigento is another notable event that marks the arrival of spring. Held in early February when the almond trees start blooming, the festival is accompanied by folk groups from all over the world, bringing dance, music, and a spirit of international friendship. The festival not only celebrates the coming of spring but also promotes peace and collaboration among different cultures.

For film enthusiasts, the Taormina Film Fest is a must-visit event. Held in the ancient Greek theatre of Taormina, this international film festival has been celebrating cinematic art since 1955. Attendees can watch a selection of international and Italian films under the stars, with the stunning backdrop of Mount Etna and the Ionian Sea. This festival combines historic scenery with contemporary cinema, creating a magical experience.

These festivals and events offer more than just entertainment; they are a gateway to understanding Sicily's soul. Participating in or even observing these festivities can provide insights into the values, traditions, and communal life of Sicilians. Each event is a reflection of the island's historical layers, cultural diversity, and the vibrant spirit of its people, making them an essential experience for any visitor seeking to truly connect with Sicily.

Cooking Classes and Wine Tasting

Sicily, with its rich culinary heritage and renowned wine culture, offers a plethora of enriching and educational experiences for food enthusiasts and oenophiles. Cooking classes and wine tastings in Sicily not only allow visitors to taste the region's gourmet offerings but also provide them with a deeper understanding of the local culture and traditions through hands-on learning and immersive experiences.

Cooking Classes

Participating in a cooking class in Sicily offers more than just a meal preparation experience; it is an invitation to delve into the heart of Sicilian family life and tradition. These classes are typically hosted by local chefs or culinary experts who are passionate about Sicilian cuisine and eager to share their knowledge. Participants learn to prepare traditional dishes such as arancini (stuffed rice balls), caponata (eggplant stew), and various pasta dishes like pasta alla Norma, which showcases the island's love for fresh, local ingredients such as tomatoes, eggplant, basil, and ricotta salata.

Many cooking classes take place in picturesque settings like old villas, farms, or traditional Sicilian kitchens, enhancing the authenticity of the experience. Some classes begin with a visit to a local market to choose fresh ingredients, where instructors teach about the seasonality and sourcing of produce and other staples of Sicilian cuisine. This market visit not only enriches the culinary experience but also introduces participants to the vibrant market culture that is central to Sicilian life.

Wine Tasting

Sicily's wine culture is as old as it is diverse, with indigenous grape varieties like Nero d'Avola and Grillo establishing the island as a formidable wine-producing region. Wine tasting tours in Sicily often take visitors through scenic vineyards, where the unique combination of volcanic soil and Mediterranean climate can be appreciated first-hand. These tours are educational, explaining the detailed processes of viticulture and winemaking, and usually end with a tasting session where the different notes and flavors of each wine are explored and discussed.

Many Sicilian wineries also offer pairing sessions, where wines are matched with local cheeses, meats, and other delicacies, allowing for a comprehensive taste experience. This not only enhances the tasting but also educates participants on how food and wine complement each other, which is a fundamental aspect of Sicilian and Italian dining culture.

Wine tours can also include historical elements, with visits to ancient cellars and estates that have been producing wine for generations. These visits often reveal the history of winemaking in the region and show how traditional methods have evolved with modern technologies.

Both cooking classes and wine tasting in Sicily offer more than just culinary delights—they provide a cultural education that engages all the senses. Participants leave with a greater appreciation of Sicilian culinary arts, understanding the deep-rooted traditions that are passed down through generations, and the pride that Sicilians take in their local produce and wine. This education in taste and tradition is what makes Sicily a truly enriching destination for anyone interested in the culinary arts.

Historical Tours

Sicily, steeped in millennia of history, offers a vast tapestry of historical narratives, each woven into the very fabric of its cities, landscapes, and archaeological sites. Historical tours in Sicily are not merely excursions; they are profound journeys through time that offer insights into the complex layers of civilizations that have shaped this Mediterranean island. These tours cater to history enthusiasts, families, scholars, and casual tourists alike, providing them with a comprehensive understanding of Sicily's past from ancient times to modern days.

cope and Diversity of Tours

Historical tours in Sicily vary widely, ranging from guided walks through ancient ruins to comprehensive trips across multiple historical sites that trace the development of Sicilian culture and architecture. These tours often focus on key periods such as the Greek, Roman, Byzantine,

Arab, Norman, and Spanish dominations, each of which has left a distinctive mark on the island.

Greek and Roman Influences

One of the highlights of historical tours in Sicily is the exploration of Greek and Roman sites. The Valley of the Temples in Agrigento is a prime example, where visitors can stroll along a ridge lined with the ruins of seven monumental Greek temples. These structures, including the well-preserved Temple of Concordia, offer a window into ancient engineering and religious life. Similarly, the ancient Roman mosaics at the Villa Romana del Casale in Piazza Armerina provide detailed insights into Roman domestic life and decor, featuring some of the most intricate and extensive mosaics found anywhere in the Roman world.

Medieval and Later Histories

Tours often extend to medieval times, where the Norman conquest of Sicily introduced a unique blend of Norman, Arab, and Byzantine influences. The Palazzo dei Normanni in Palermo, with its stunning Palatine Chapel, showcases the opulence of Norman rulers and their eclectic artistic tastes. Furthermore, the tour might include a visit to the cathedral of Monreale, renowned for its breathtaking Byzantine mosaics and Romanesque architecture.

Cultural Integration
Beyond mere architectural and historical education, many tours also delve into the cultural aspects of Sicilian history, illustrating how the island's geographical position has made it a melting pot of cultures. This aspect is particularly palpable in cities like Syracuse, where ancient Greek ruins stand alongside medieval lanes and baroque churches, reflecting a timeline of occupation and integration that has contributed to the rich cultural tapestry of the island.

Specialized Historical Tours

For those with specific interests, Sicily offers specialized tours such as those focusing on the Baroque cities of the Val di Noto, including Ragusa, Modica, and Noto itself, each rebuilt in grand Baroque style after the devastating earthquake of 1693. These cities are UNESCO World Heritage sites and are celebrated for their artistic and architectural significance.

Interactive and Educational Components

To enhance the educational value, many historical tours in Sicily incorporate interactive elements such as reenactments, multimedia presentations, and guided talks that engage visitors in the historical narrative. These components are particularly valuable for educational groups or families with children, making history accessible and engaging for all ages. Historical tours in Sicily offer more than just sightseeing; they provide a deep dive into the events and people who have shaped the island's history. Through these tours, visitors gain a profound appreciation of Sicily's historical importance in the Mediterranean world, its cultural diversity, and its enduring influence across centuries. Each site visited and story told is part of a larger narrative that continues to fascinate and educate those who walk the island's ancient paths.

CHAPTER 10

Practical Information

Navigating the practical aspects of travel in Sicily is crucial for ensuring a smooth and enjoyable experience. This chapter provides essential information tailored to help tourists understand and manage the logistical and practical elements of their visit to this magnificent island. From transportation tips and accommodation advice to insights on local customs and communication essentials, this section is designed to equip you with the knowledge needed to navigate Sicily with confidence.

Transportation in Sicily offers various options, and understanding these can significantly enhance your travel experience. Whether you're planning to explore the bustling streets of Palermo, the ancient ruins of Agrigento, or the picturesque landscapes of the Sicilian countryside, knowing how to effectively use public transport, rental services, or when to opt for guided tours can make a difference in how you experience the island.

Accommodations in Sicily range from luxurious hotels and resorts to charming B&Bs and budget-friendly hostels. This chapter will guide you through choosing the right type of stay that not only fits your budget but also positions you conveniently for the activities you plan to enjoy. Plus, tips on securing the best deals and what to expect during peak and off-peak seasons will be covered to help you plan your trip strategically.

Understanding local customs and etiquette is another vital aspect that can enrich your interaction with Sicilians and enhance your overall travel experience. Sicily prides itself on a rich cultural heritage and warm hospitality, and knowing a few local customs can go a long way in fostering respectful and engaging interactions.

Additionally, this chapter will delve into practical advice on communication, including common phrases in Italian that tourists might find useful, tips on connectivity options like mobile data and Wi-Fi availability, and the locations of essential services like pharmacies, hospitals, and tourist information centers.

This practical information is not merely logistical but is aimed at weaving these details into the larger tapestry of your Sicilian adventure, ensuring that you are well-prepared to dive deep into the island's offerings without being bogged down by uncertainties or logistical oversights. Whether you are savoring a glass of Nero d'Avola in a seaside restaurant or hiking the rugged paths of Mount Etna, the insights provided here will help ensure that your focus remains on the rich experiences Sicily has to offer.

Currency, Banking, and ATMs

Understanding the basics of currency, banking, and ATMs is crucial for any traveler visiting Sicily, ensuring smooth financial transactions and avoiding any potential inconveniences during your stay. This section provides comprehensive insights into the financial infrastructure of Sicily, from the type of currency used to practical tips on accessing your funds while exploring this vibrant island.

Currency

Sicily uses the Euro (€) as its official currency, which is common across most European countries. This uniformity makes it easier for travelers coming from other Eurozone countries, as they do not need to exchange their money. For travelers from outside the Eurozone, it's advisable to exchange some amount of currency into Euros before arriving or upon arrival.

Exchanging Money

Currency can be exchanged at various points throughout Sicily, including banks, post offices, and dedicated exchange bureaus found in major airports and tourist areas. While exchange bureaus offer the convenience of extended operating hours and immediate service, they often come with higher fees and less favorable exchange rates compared to banks. Therefore, planning ahead and knowing where to exchange money can save you both time and expenses.

Banking Services

Sicily has a robust banking system with branches of both national and international banks available, especially in larger cities like Palermo, Catania, and Messina. These banks provide a full range of services including currency exchange, international transfers, and financial advice. Banking hours typically run from Monday to Friday, 8:30 AM to 1:30 PM, and then from around 3:00 PM to 4:00 PM. Most banks are closed on weekends, so it's essential to plan your banking activities accordingly.

ATMs

ATMs, locally known as 'Bancomat', are widely available throughout Sicily, including in smaller towns. They are often the most convenient way to withdraw cash as they operate 24/7. Most ATMs in Sicily accept international debit and credit cards, making them a viable option for immediate cash needs. However, it's important to be aware of possible fees for international transactions, which can vary depending on your bank's policies and the ATM used.

Safety Tips

When using ATMs, always ensure maximum privacy by covering the keypad when entering your PIN and be aware of your surroundings, especially if withdrawing money at night. It is also advisable to use ATMs attached to banks for added security and easier assistance in case the machine malfunctions or retains your card.

Practical Tips:
1. Inform your home bank of your travel plans to avoid any interruptions in service due to suspicious foreign transactions.
2. Carry a mix of payment options such as cash, debit cards, and credit cards to ensure you're covered in different situations.
3. Keep small change handy for everyday expenses such as public transportation and street food, as small vendors may not accept credit cards.
4. Download a reliable currency conversion app on your mobile device to help you understand prices and manage your spending efficiently.

Connectivity: SIM Cards and Internet Access

Staying connected while traveling in Sicily is crucial for both practical reasons and for sharing your experiences with friends and family back home. This comprehensive guide discusses the various options for securing SIM cards and accessing the internet, ensuring that you remain connected smoothly and affordably throughout your stay in Sicily.

SIM Cards

For tourists visiting Sicily, purchasing a local SIM card can be a cost-effective way to access mobile services, including calls, texts, and, most importantly, data. Several mobile operators in Italy offer prepaid SIM cards that are well-suited for short-term visitors, including TIM, Vodafone, Wind, and Tre. These can be purchased at airports, kiosks, and dedicated stores in major cities and tourist areas across Sicily.

When buying a SIM card, you will need a valid form of identification, such as a passport. The staff at the point of purchase will usually help set up the SIM card, ensuring that it is functioning correctly before you leave the store. It's important to choose a plan that matches your expected usage; most operators offer various options tailored to different needs, such as packages with ample data allowances which are particularly useful for navigating maps, using translation apps, and regular internet browsing.

Internet Access

In addition to mobile data, Sicily offers widespread access to Wi-Fi in various public spaces, accommodations, and eateries. Most hotels, guesthouses, and Airbnb rentals provide free Wi-Fi to their guests. However, the quality of the connection can vary, especially in remote areas or smaller establishments, so it's wise to check reviews or confirm with hosts about internet reliability if online access is crucial during your stay. For those needing more consistent internet access, many cafes and restaurants also provide free Wi-Fi to customers. Places like McDonald's, Starbucks, and local cafés are often reliable spots to get connected. Keep an eye out for signs indicating Wi-Fi availability, or simply ask the staff for the network name and password. Moreover, several towns and cities in Sicily have initiated projects to offer free public Wi-Fi in main squares, parks, and public buildings. While the connection speed might not always be high due to the number of users, it's sufficient for basic browsing and checking emails.

Practical Tips for Connectivity

1. Consider Unlocking Your Phone: Before traveling, ensure your phone is unlocked so that it can accept a foreign SIM card. This can usually be arranged through your current provider.

2. Check the Coverage: Before purchasing a SIM card, check the coverage map provided by the operator, especially if you plan to visit rural or isolated areas of Sicily.

3. Use Messaging Apps: To save on call and SMS costs, use internet-based messaging apps like WhatsApp, Messenger, or Skype for communicating with friends and family.

4. Data Security: When using public Wi-Fi networks, consider using a virtual private network (VPN) to secure your data from potential threats.

5. Download Offline Maps and Guides: To save on data usage, download offline maps and travel guides before you leave your accommodation.

Understanding these aspects of connectivity ensures that you stay in touch, navigate efficiently, and make the most of your travel experience in Sicily without facing unexpected hurdles.

Emergency Contacts and Useful Numbers

When traveling to Sicily, having knowledge of emergency contacts and useful numbers is crucial for addressing any unexpected situations swiftly and efficiently. This comprehensive guide provides a detailed list of essential contacts, ensuring that travelers can access help whenever necessary, from medical emergencies to legal assistance and more.

Emergency Services

The most important number to remember is **112**, the pan-European emergency number, which can be dialed free of charge from any phone. This number connects callers to emergency services for police, fire, and medical assistance. Operators are equipped to respond to calls in multiple languages, making it accessible for tourists who do not speak Italian.

Medical Emergencies

For medical emergencies, apart from the general 112 number, you can directly call **118**. This connects to the emergency medical services where immediate medical response teams are dispatched. It is also advisable to know the locations and contact numbers of the nearest hospitals and pharmacies in the area you are staying. Pharmacies in Sicily are well-equipped and pharmacists often speak enough English to provide advice on minor ailments or recommend over-the-counter medications.

Police Assistance

For non-urgent police assistance, dial **113**. This number is useful for reporting crimes that aren't currently in progress or for seeking police intervention without the immediate urgency that warrants a 112 call.

Fire Brigade

In the event of a fire, dial **115** to reach the fire brigade. This service is not only for fighting fires but also for dealing with accidents where people are trapped and other emergencies like flooding or gas leaks.

Coast Guard

Given Sicily's extensive coastline, knowing the number for the coast guard is essential. You can contact the coast guard by dialing **1530**. This service is crucial for reporting any sea-related incidents or emergencies.

Consular Assistance

Travelers should also have the contact details of their respective embassies or consulates. While specific numbers vary by country, all diplomatic missions provide assistance to their citizens in cases of legal troubles, lost passports, or other serious issues while abroad.

Roadside Assistance

If you are traveling by car, it is practical to have contact details for roadside assistance. The

Automobile Club d'Italia (ACI) provides help for motorists in distress, and they can be reached at **116**. This service can prove invaluable in case of a breakdown or accident.

Useful Tips for Handling Emergencies

1. **Carry a list of emergency contacts both digitally and physically**: Sometimes, access to digital devices might be restricted, and having a physical copy ensures you have the information when needed.

2. **Inform someone of your daily itinerary:** Whether it's your hotel reception or a family member back home, let someone know of your plans, especially if you are venturing into remote areas.

3. **Download a translation app:** This can be invaluable in communicating with local services if you do not speak Italian.

4. **Travel insurance:** Always travel with insurance that covers medical and travel-related emergencies. Know the terms and have the contact details for claims handy.

By being prepared with these essential contacts and tips, travelers can ensure that they are equipped to handle any situation that may arise during their stay in Sicily, allowing them to focus more on enjoying their visit to this culturally and historically rich island.

CHAPTER 11

Packing List

Preparing for a trip to Sicily involves thoughtful consideration of what to pack, ensuring that you are well-equipped for the diverse activities and climates the island offers throughout the year. This chapter is designed to provide you with a comprehensive packing list that caters to Sicily's unique weather patterns, cultural norms, and the variety of experiences you may encounter, from exploring ancient archaeological sites and engaging in outdoor activities to dining at upscale restaurants and strolling through bustling markets.

Sicily experiences a Mediterranean climate, with hot, dry summers and mild, wet winters. Depending on the season of your visit, your packing list will vary significantly. For summer travels, lightweight clothing, sun hats, and sturdy sandals are essential for comfort and protection against the Sicilian sun. Conversely, visiting in the cooler months requires layers, including a warm jacket and long pants, to adapt to the variable temperatures, especially in the evenings or when exploring higher altitudes like Mount Etna.

Beyond clothing, there are several other essentials to consider. Comfortable walking shoes are a must for navigating the cobblestone streets of historic towns and hiking in natural parks. Sunscreen, sunglasses, and a reusable water bottle are crucial for daily excursions. Additionally, cultural sensitivity and respect for local customs suggest modest attire when visiting religious sites, so including items that can cover shoulders and knees is advisable.

Furthermore, this chapter will cover technological needs and conveniences, such as adapters for Sicily's electrical outlets, portable chargers, and tips on choosing the right travel bags to secure your belongings while on the move. We'll also touch on the importance of packing any necessary medications and health-related items, alongside travel documents and security measures to keep them safe.

Overall, the aim is to ensure that your suitcase contains everything needed for a comfortable, enjoyable, and respectful visit to Sicily. This guide will help streamline your packing process, reduce the likelihood of overpacking, and ensure that you are prepared for the many adventures that await in this enchanting region. With the right items in your luggage, you'll be free to immerse yourself fully in the Sicilian experience, capturing memories without the hassle of unpreparedness.

Seasonal Packing Tips

Packing for a trip to Sicily requires consideration of the island's diverse climates and seasonal variations, ensuring that you are well-prepared for its varying weather patterns and local activities. Whether visiting the sun-soaked beaches during summer or exploring ancient archaeological sites in the cooler months, understanding how to pack for each season is crucial. This guide provides detailed advice on how to tailor your packing list to Sicily's seasons, ensuring comfort, practicality, and respect for local customs.

Spring (March to May)

Spring in Sicily is marked by gradually warming temperatures and a landscape bursting into bloom. This is an ideal time for sightseeing as the weather is comfortable and not yet as hot as in summer. Packing should include layers that can be adjusted easily. Lightweight sweaters, long-sleeve shirts, and a medium-weight jacket are perfect for the cooler mornings and evenings. Include comfortable walking shoes, as this is a great time to explore outdoor markets and hillside villages. Don't forget a light rain jacket or an umbrella, as spring can occasionally bring showers.

Summer (June to August)

Summer in Sicily is hot and dry, making it perfect for beach activities but potentially challenging for extended outdoor sightseeing in urban areas. Essentials include lightweight, breathable clothing—think linen and cotton in light colors to reflect the sun's rays. A wide-brimmed hat, high-SPF sunscreen, and sunglasses are crucial to protect against the sun. Pack a swimsuit, a beach towel, and flip-flops for coastal activities, along with a sturdy pair of sandals for walking on hot, cobblestone streets. Remember to include a cover-up or a sarong for visits to churches and religious sites where modest attire is required.

Autumn (September to November)

Autumn sees the return of milder temperatures and the start of the grape harvest, making it a fantastic season for visiting vineyards. The weather can be variable, ranging from warm to cool, so packing layers is again advisable. Include items such as T-shirts, long-sleeve tops, light sweaters, and a comfortable jacket. This is also a great time for hiking in Sicily's natural parks, so durable walking shoes and a waterproof jacket are recommended. As the evenings can be cool, bring along a medium-weight jacket.

Winter (December to February)

Sicilian winters are generally mild compared to northern Europe, but it can still be quite cool, especially in the evenings and in the mountainous areas. Pack warm clothing including sweaters, long pants, and a heavier jacket or coat. If planning to visit Mount Etna or other high-altitude locations, consider thermal wear, a warm hat, gloves, and a scarf. Footwear should be waterproof and suitable for potentially rainy weather. Despite the cooler temperatures, winter in Sicily is filled with vibrant festivities, so pack some smart-casual outfits for attending events or dining out.

General Tips
- Adaptability: Choose clothing that can be layered easily, allowing for adjustments based on the day's activities and weather changes.
- Footwear: Comfortable shoes are a must, as exploring Sicily often involves a lot of walking. Consider the terrain and season when selecting shoes.
- Cultural Sensitivity: Always include modest clothing options for visiting religious sites.
- Accessories: Bring a daypack for day trips and excursions, and consider a portable charger for your devices, as you'll be taking lots of photos.

Must-Have Items for Sicily

When planning a trip to Sicily, certain items are essential to include in your luggage to ensure a comfortable and hassle-free experience. This comprehensive guide highlights the must-have items for your Sicilian adventure, tailored to accommodate the island's varied landscapes, climates, and cultural experiences. Ensuring you pack these items will not only enhance your convenience but also enrich your engagement with the diverse attractions Sicily has to offer.

1. **Sun Protection Gear:** Given Sicily's Mediterranean climate, sun protection is paramount. A high SPF sunscreen, sunglasses with UV protection, and a wide-brimmed hat are essential to shield yourself from the sun, particularly during the summer months when UV levels are at their highest. Sunscreen should be reapplied regularly, especially after swimming or sweating.

2. Comfortable Footwear: Whether exploring the ancient ruins of Agrigento's Valley of the Temples or wandering the cobbled streets of Taormina, comfortable and sturdy footwear is crucial. Opt for breathable, well-cushioned walking shoes for daytime exploration. Sandals may be suitable for beach days, while a more formal pair of shoes can be useful for evening dining as Sicilians often dress stylishly.

3. Appropriate Clothing: Layering is key when packing for Sicily. Lightweight, breathable fabrics work well for the warm weather, while a light sweater or pashmina can be useful for cooler evenings or modest dress requirements when visiting religious sites. Including a waterproof jacket or umbrella is wise, especially outside of the summer season when showers are more common.

4. Daypack: A small, comfortable backpack or daypack is invaluable for day trips. It should be large enough to carry water, snacks, a travel guide, your camera, and any souvenirs you might pick up along the way. Consider a theft-proof backpack with lockable zippers for added security while in crowded areas.

5. Water Bottle: Staying hydrated is important in the Sicilian heat. Carrying a reusable water bottle is environmentally friendly and economical, as you can refill it throughout the day at your accommodation or at public water fountains found in some towns.

6. Health and Safety Items: A basic travel health kit should include medication for common ailments such as headaches, stomach upsets, and allergies, as well as plasters and antiseptic for minor cuts and scrapes. Also, keep a copy of any prescriptions and a list of emergency contacts.

7. Power Adapter and Charger: Italy uses Type L power sockets, so a suitable adapter is necessary to charge electronic devices. Additionally, a portable power bank can be handy for long days out when access to a power outlet might be limited.

8. Travel Documents and Copies: Ensure you carry your passport, ID, travel insurance details, and any booking confirmations. It's also prudent to keep a digital and physical copy of these important documents in a separate location from the originals.

9. Language Guide or App: While many Sicilians speak some English, particularly in tourist areas, having a basic Italian phrasebook or a translation app can enhance your interactions with locals and enrich your travel experience.

10. Camera or Smartphone: Lastly, don't forget a camera or smartphone with ample memory to capture the scenic vistas, historic sites, and vibrant street scenes. Sicily's picturesque landscapes are worth documenting and sharing.

CHAPTER 12

Itineraries

Exploring Sicily, with its rich tapestry of history, culture, and natural beauty, can be an overwhelming experience if you don't know where to start. This chapter on itineraries is designed to help you make the most of your visit, whether you have just a day to spare or an entire week to delve deep into the island's offerings. Each suggested itinerary is crafted to ensure a comprehensive and enriching Sicilian experience, tailored to different lengths of stay and interests.

Our itineraries guide you through the bustling streets of Palermo, the ancient ruins of Agrigento, and the serene landscapes of the Sicilian countryside, providing a balanced mix of historical sites, cultural encounters, and natural wonders. For those on a short visit, we outline efficient day trips and excursions that capture the essence of Sicily, focusing on can't-miss attractions and local dining experiences. For travelers with more time, our extended itineraries offer a deeper exploration of the island, with opportunities to immerse yourself in the local lifestyle, participate in traditional festivals, and perhaps venture off the beaten path to discover Sicily's hidden gems.

Each itinerary also includes practical tips on transportation, the best times to visit specific locations, and recommendations for authentic Sicilian eateries and accommodations. By structuring your travel plans with these itineraries, you can enjoy a seamless and fulfilling journey through Sicily, ensuring that you leave with a rich collection of memories and a deep appreciation of this enchanting island. Whether you're a history enthusiast, a lover of nature, or a culinary aficionado, these itineraries are designed to give you a profound connection to Sicily's diverse attractions.

Day Trips and Excursions

Sicily, a treasure trove of cultural heritage and natural beauty, offers an abundance of options for day trips and excursions that allow visitors to capture the essence of the island in short, manageable adventures. These activities are designed to showcase the diversity of Sicily's landscapes, historical sites, and cultural experiences, providing travelers with a taste of everything from ancient archaeological sites to picturesque coastal towns.

Exploring Ancient Ruins

One of the most compelling day trips in Sicily involves visiting the Valley of the Temples in Agrigento. This UNESCO World Heritage site is home to some of the best-preserved Greek temples outside of Greece. A guided tour can enrich your visit by providing historical context and insights into the lives of the ancient Sicilians who built these magnificent structures. The archaeological park opens early in the morning, which is the best time to explore before the midday sun intensifies.

Vibrant Coastal Towns

Another excellent day trip option is to explore the vibrant coastal towns of Sicily, such as Cefalù or Taormina. Cefalù offers a charming blend of medieval streets, sandy beaches, and the stunning backdrop of La Rocca. You can spend the morning wandering through the town's historical center and the afternoon relaxing by the sea. Taormina, on the other hand, is famous for its ancient Greek theater and breathtaking views of Mount Etna and the Ionian coast. It's a perfect spot for those who appreciate history intertwined with scenic beauty.

Mount Etna Adventures

For those inclined towards nature and adventure, a trip to Mount Etna, Europe's largest and most active volcano, is a must. Various tour companies offer guided excursions that can include hiking to some of the lower craters, cable car rides to higher altitudes, and even jeep tours around the rugged terrain of the volcanic landscape. These tours not only provide a safe way to experience the grandeur of Etna but also offer insights into its geological significance and the impact on the local environment.

Food and Wine Tasting Tours

Sicily is also renowned for its culinary delights, and no visit is complete without indulging in a food and wine tasting tour. These excursions often take you through local markets, vineyards, and rural farms where traditional methods are still in use. For instance, a visit to a winery on the slopes of Mount Etna not only offers tastings of unique volcanic wines but also includes samplings of local cheeses, olives, and cured meats, all produced in the rich soils of the region.

Cultural Immersion

For a deeper cultural experience, consider a day trip focused on Sicilian crafts and traditions. Towns like Erice and Modica not only boast incredible medieval architecture but are also centers for traditional crafts such as ceramic pottery and chocolate making, respectively. Participating in workshops or demonstrations can provide a hands-on understanding of these age-old crafts.

Each of these day trips and excursions is designed to offer a unique perspective of Sicily, catering to different interests whether they lie in history, nature, gastronomy, or culture. By carefully planning these short trips, you ensure that even a brief visit is filled with enriching experiences that paint a comprehensive picture of what Sicily has to offer. Moreover, these outings emphasize the island's rich tapestry of influences, from the ancient to the modern, making every excursion a learning opportunity and an adventure.

3-Day Itineraries

Crafting a 3-day itinerary in Sicily allows travelers to immerse themselves in the rich tapestry of Sicilian culture, history, and natural beauty without the rush that shorter trips often entail. This extended timeframe provides a golden opportunity to explore a blend of Sicily's best offerings—from ancient ruins and majestic landscapes to vibrant markets and culinary delights. Here, we outline a comprehensive 3-day journey designed to captivate and educate, ensuring travelers leave with a profound appreciation of this enchanting island.

Day 1: Palermo and Monreale

Begin your Sicilian adventure in Palermo, the capital city, rich in history and culture. Spend your morning exploring the Palermo Cathedral, with its impressive architecture that tells tales of the city's diverse cultural influences. Walk through the bustling markets like Ballarò or Vucciria, where you can taste local street food specialties such as panelle (chickpea fritters) and arancini (rice balls).

In the afternoon, take a short drive to Monreale, a town famous for its stunning Norman Cathedral, adorned with golden mosaics depicting biblical stories. This site not only provides insight into the Norman conquest of Sicily but also showcases the island's unique blend of Norman and Byzantine art. Return to Palermo for an evening stroll along the marina or enjoy a traditional Sicilian dinner at a local trattoria.

Day 2: Agrigento and the Valley of the Temples
On the second day, head to Agrigento, one of Sicily's oldest cities, and visit the Valley of the Temples, a UNESCO World Heritage site. This archaeological marvel features some of the best-preserved Greek temples outside of Greece. The highlight is the Temple of Concordia, whose ancient columns rise dramatically against the backdrop of the Sicilian countryside.

Dedicate the afternoon to exploring the less crowded parts of the site, such as the Temple of Hera and the ancient olive groves. Learn about the site's extensive history through a guided tour, which can provide deeper insight into the significance of each structure and the daily lives of the ancient Greeks in Sicily.

Day 3: Mount Etna and Taormina

On your final day, venture to Mount Etna, Europe's largest and most active volcano. Participating in a guided tour up the volcano offers not only safety but also educational commentary about Etna's geological importance and its impact on the local environment. The adventurous can hike to some of the lesser craters, while others might prefer a cable car ride to get panoramic views without the exertion.

In the afternoon, drive to Taormina, a charming town perched on a cliff overlooking the Ionian

Sea. Visit the ancient Greco-Roman theatre, which offers spectacular views of Mount Etna and the coast below. Spend the rest of your day wandering through Taormina's quaint streets, visiting its boutiques and enjoying gelato from a local gelateria.

This 3-day itinerary provides a balanced experience of Sicily's rich historical tapestry, vibrant culture, and breathtaking natural landscapes. Each day is structured to offer an educational journey through time and space, from the ancient streets of Palermo to the volcanic heights of Etna, leaving travelers enriched and inspired. By focusing on key highlights, this itinerary ensures that visitors can engage deeply with each location, gaining insights and memories that resonate long after the journey ends.

7-Day Itineraries

A 7-day itinerary in Sicily offers a comprehensive journey through the island's rich mosaic of history, culture, landscapes, and culinary delights. This extended stay allows for a deeper exploration of Sicily's most cherished sights alongside hidden gems, providing a well-rounded experience of what the island has to offer. Here's how to make the most of a week in this Mediterranean paradise, presented in a seamless narrative that ensures you soak in every aspect of Sicilian life.

Day 1: Arrival and Palermo
Begin your Sicilian adventure in Palermo, the vibrant capital of the island. Spend your first day acclimating to the local pace and exploring the historic city center. Key attractions include the Palermo Cathedral and the Palazzo dei Normanni, the oldest royal residence in Europe. In the evening, dive into Palermo's street food culture at the bustling markets of La Vucciria or Ballarò,

where you can sample local specialties like sfincione (Sicilian pizza) and cannoli.

Day 2: Monreale and Cefalù

Travel to Monreale to visit its stunning cathedral, famous for the breathtaking mosaics depicting biblical stories. Afterward, head to the coastal town of Cefalù. Wander the medieval streets, relax on the beach, and climb La Rocca for spectacular views over the town and coast.

Day 3: The Greek Ruins of Agrigento

Drive to Agrigento to explore the Valley of the Temples, an archaeological site that ranks among the most important in the world. Take a guided tour to learn about the magnificent ruins of ancient Akragas, and spend the afternoon visiting the nearby Garden of Kolymbetra, an ancient garden recently restored to its historical splendor.

Day 4: Villa Romana del Casale and Ragusa

Visit the Villa Romana del Casale near Piazza Armerina, home to some of the best-preserved Roman mosaics in the world. Then, continue to Ragusa, a city known for its Baroque architecture. Explore Ragusa Ibla, the old town, with its beautiful churches and palaces.

Day 5: Syracuse and Ortigia
Head to Syracuse to delve into its ancient Greek history. Visit the archaeological park featuring the Greek theater, the Roman amphitheater, and the Ear of Dionysius. Spend the afternoon and evening on the island of Ortigia, where you can see the stunning Duomo and enjoy a waterside dinner.

Day 6: Mount Etna and Taormina
Experience the natural wonder of Mount Etna. Depending on your interest and ability, you can take a cable car, a 4x4 bus, or even hike to one of the summit craters. In the afternoon, drive to Taormina, Sicily's chic cliffside town. Visit the

ancient Greek theatre and enjoy some leisure time strolling through the charming streets or relaxing at a café.

Day 7: Taormina and Departure
Spend your last day relaxing in Taormina. Take a morning walk through the public gardens and do some last-minute shopping for local delicacies and crafts. As your trip comes to a close, reflect on the rich experiences of the past week, from the stunning architecture and profound history to the breathtaking landscapes and vibrant local life of Sicily.

This 7-day itinerary is crafted not just to move through locations, but to experience them deeply, allowing for cultural immersion, historical exploration, and personal leisure. Each day builds on the last, providing a narrative thread that connects you to the diverse and dynamic spirit of Sicily, ensuring that your time spent here is not just memorable, but truly transformative.

CHAPTER 13

Helpful Resources

Embarking on a journey through Sicily offers an exciting array of experiences, but navigating a new place effectively often requires access to a variety of helpful resources. This chapter is dedicated to providing you with an array of tools and information designed to enhance your travel experience across the island. From understanding the geography that shapes this vibrant land to selecting the most reliable car rental services and finding the best guided tours, this section serves as your comprehensive guide to accessing essential services and information.

As you dive into this chapter, you will discover detailed insights into the most accurate and user-friendly geographic tools to help you appreciate Sicily's diverse landscapes. Whether you're planning a route through the bustling streets of Palermo or a scenic drive along the coast, the resources outlined here will ensure you have the necessary information at your fingertips.

Moreover, for those considering car rentals, we provide tips on choosing the right provider, understanding local driving laws, and recommendations for making the most of your road trips around the island. Additionally, if you prefer a more structured exploration, we'll introduce you to reputable guided tour companies that offer a range of options from historical excursions to culinary adventures.

To further assist your journey, we explore a variety of apps and tools that can enhance communication, navigation, and cultural engagement. Each suggested resource has been carefully selected for its reliability and ease of use, ensuring that you can focus more on enjoying your visit and less on logistics. This chapter is designed not just to inform but also to empower you as a traveler, providing the necessary tools to navigate Sicily with confidence and curiosity. Here, you'll find everything needed to turn a good holiday into a great adventure, filled with the rich textures of Sicilian life and landscapes.

The Geography of Sicily

Sicily, a gem of the Mediterranean, boasts a geography as dynamic and diverse as its history. This island, the largest in the Mediterranean Sea, serves as a natural bridge between Europe and Africa, positioned just off the southern tip of Italy, separated by the narrow Strait of Messina. Sicily's geographical features have shaped its culture, economy, and lifestyle throughout history, making a profound impact on the identity and development of the island.

Topography and Natural Landscapes:

Sicily's topography is predominantly mountainous, with rolling hills that foster a variety of natural habitats and agricultural environments. The island is famously home to Mount Etna, one of the most active volcanoes in the world, standing at about 3,329 meters (10,922 feet) high. Etna is not only a central figure in the island's geography but also in its agricultural practices, as the volcanic soil is exceptionally fertile, supporting the cultivation of vineyards and orchards that produce world-renowned wines and citrus fruits.

The northeast features the Nebrodi and Madonie mountain ranges, part of the Apennine chain, which are less rugged than the volcanic areas but equally significant in shaping the local climate and biodiversity. These mountains are lush and green, home to a variety of flora and fauna, and offer stunning vistas of the Tyrrhenian Sea.

Coastal Geography

Sicily is encircled by nearly 1,000 kilometers of coastline, varied from sandy beaches to rocky cliffs. The northern coast is characterized by dramatic cliffs and has fewer beaches, while the southern and eastern coasts are lined with wide sandy stretches like those found in the famous beach towns of Cefalù and Taormina. The variety in the coastline not only makes Sicily a prime destination for beach lovers but also affects local weather patterns and has historically influenced maritime activities and trade.

Islands and Archipelagos

Around Sicily, several smaller islands and archipelagos, including the Aeolian Islands to the northeast, the Egadi Islands to the west, and Pantelleria and the Pelagie Islands to the south, form part of its provinces. These islands, each with unique geological and cultural features, contribute to the diversity of Sicily's landscape and are integral to its maritime identity.

Rivers and Natural Resources

Sicily's river systems are mostly seasonal, fed by the winter rains but often dry in the summer months. The most significant rivers include the Simeto, which flows into the Ionian Sea, and the Belice, flowing to the south coast. These waterways are crucial for the agricultural sectors, particularly in cultivating the island's famous oranges, lemons, and olives.

Climate Impact:

The geography of Sicily directly influences its climate, which is typically Mediterranean with hot, dry summers and mild, wet winters. This climate allows for the cultivation of a rich variety of crops, including grapes, olives, citrus fruits, and almonds, which are essential to Sicilian cuisine and export.

Understanding the geography of Sicily provides valuable insights into the natural beauty and resources of the island, explaining much about the lifestyles and traditions of its people. From the high peaks of Mount Etna to the rich waters surrounding its coasts, Sicily's geographical diversity is a fundamental part of what makes the island so uniquely captivating.

The Climate of Sicily

The climate of Sicily, like its landscapes, is richly varied and plays a pivotal role in the daily life, agriculture, and tourist activities on the island. Understanding the climatic patterns of Sicily not only enriches the travel experience but also provides insight into the seasonal activities and cultural events you can expect during your visit.

Mediterranean Climate

Sicily experiences a typical Mediterranean climate characterized by hot, dry summers and mild, wet winters. This climate pattern is influenced by the island's geographical position in the central Mediterranean Sea, which acts as a buffer against extreme weather changes and helps maintain relatively moderate temperatures throughout the year.

Summer Season (June to August)

Summers in Sicily are renowned for their warmth and sunshine, making it a popular season for beach tourism. Daytime temperatures often rise above 30°C (86°F), with minimal rainfall. The warm weather is ideal for enjoying Sicily's extensive coastlines and is conducive to the long, leisurely dining experiences that are a staple of Sicilian culture. However, the high temperatures also necessitate precautions against sun exposure, including hydration and sun protection.

Autumn Season (September to November)

Autumn in Sicily sees a gradual cooling, with temperatures ranging from 25°C (77°F) in early September to around 15°C (59°F) by late November. This season is often considered one of the best times to visit due to the milder weather and the decrease in tourist crowds. Rainfall begins to increase, particularly in November, which rejuvenates the countryside and marks the beginning of the agricultural planting season.

Winter Season (December to February)

Winters are mild compared to much of Europe, with coastal temperatures averaging around 10°C to 15°C (50°F to 59°F). Inland and mountainous areas, particularly those at higher altitudes near Mount Etna, can experience cooler temperatures and even snow. Winter is also the wettest season, which is crucial for replenishing Sicily's water reserves and supporting the growth of crops such as citrus fruits, which are harvested in the winter months.

Spring Season (March to May)

Spring is heralded by a beautiful bloom across the island's diverse flora, with temperatures gradually rising from cool to warm. This season is characterized by occasional rain showers and increasing sunshine, with average temperatures ranging from 15°C (59°F) in March to about 25°C (77°F) by May. Spring is an excellent time for agricultural tours and outdoor activities, as the island is lush and green, and the weather is comfortable for exploring.

Local Microclimates

Due to its varied topography, Sicily also exhibits several microclimates. The highlands around Mount Etna can be significantly cooler than the coastal areas, and the smaller islands around Sicily may experience slightly different weather patterns due to their maritime influences.

Understanding Sicily's climate is essential for planning travel and activities, as it affects everything from what to pack to the best times for visiting specific attractions or participating in local festivals. The pleasant climate year-round makes Sicily a versatile destination, offering something special in every season, driven by both its natural environmental rhythm and the vibrant Sicilian culture that embraces and adapts to these seasonal shifts.

Car Rentals and Navigating on Your Own

Renting a car and navigating on your own in Sicily offers a flexible and intimate way to explore the island, giving you the freedom to discover its varied landscapes, historic sites, and hidden gems at your own pace. This guide provides you with essential information on how to rent a car, navigate the Sicilian roads, and make the most of your self-directed travels across this diverse Mediterranean island.

Car Rental Basics

When renting a car in Sicily, you'll find numerous options available at airports, in major cities, and through various online platforms. It's advisable to book your vehicle in advance, especially during peak tourist seasons, to ensure availability and better rates. Requirements typically include a valid driver's license from your home country, and often an international driving permit (IDP), as well as a credit card for a security deposit.

Make sure to choose a vehicle that suits the nature of your travel. Compact cars are ideal for navigating the narrow streets of Sicilian towns and villages, while a vehicle with good road grip and power might be better if you plan to explore the mountainous regions. Additionally, fully understand your rental agreement, paying close attention to insurance coverage, mileage limits, and fuel policy.

Navigating Sicilian Roads

Driving in Sicily can be challenging but rewarding. The island's roads range from well-maintained highways (autostrade) to winding rural roads that offer stunning scenic views but may require careful handling. Major highways connect big cities like Palermo, Catania, and Messina, and are the quickest way to traverse long distances. However, the real charm of Sicily often lies off the beaten path. Exploring smaller roads requires a bit more patience and skill, especially in the hilly or mountainous areas. It's essential to be prepared for a driving style that can seem aggressive to those not used to Southern Italian traffic norms. Defensive driving and a good navigation system or GPS app can help you manage the roads more confidently.

Local Traffic Laws and Regulations

Familiarize yourself with local traffic laws. In Sicily, as in all of Italy, you drive on the right-hand side of the road. Speed limits are typically 50 km/h in urban areas, 90 km/h on secondary rural roads, and 130 km/h on highways, unless different speeds are posted. Seat belts are mandatory for all passengers, and the use of mobile phones while driving is prohibited unless you have a hands-free system.

Parking in Sicilian cities can be particularly challenging. Many urban areas have restricted traffic zones (Zona Traffico Limitato, or ZTL) which require special permits to enter during certain hours. Always check signs for parking regulations to avoid fines and take note of the color-coded parking lines: white for free parking, blue for paid parking, and yellow for restricted parking.

Benefits of Self-Driving:
Having your own vehicle allows you to stop at lesser-known sites, take spontaneous detours, and spend as much time as you like in places that interest you. You can start early to avoid crowds at popular destinations like the Valley of the Temples, or linger for sunset views over the Mediterranean from a quiet coastal spot. Renting a car in Sicily enhances your travel experience by providing the freedom to explore the island at your own pace, from its bustling cities to its serene countryside. Below are several reputable car rental agencies in Sicily, offering a range of vehicles to suit different travel needs and budgets. This list includes their contact information, ensuring you can make reservations easily and

receive the best possible service during your Sicilian adventure.

1. Sicily by Car
- **Location:** Palermo Airport, Palermo
- **Phone:** +39 091 591688
- **Email:** info@sicilybycar.it
- **Website:** (http://www.sicilybycar.it)
- **Price Range:** $30 - $100 per day, depending on the car model and season.

2. AutoEuropa
- **Location:** Via Francesco Crispi, 260, 95128 Catania CT, Sicily
- **Phone:** +39 095 346893
- **Email:** customer.service@autoeuropa.it
- **Website:** (http://www.autoeuropa.it)
- **Price Range:** $25 - $90 per day, which varies with car type and rental duration.

3. Avis Car Rental

- **Location:** Via Luigi Pirandello, 35C, 90141 Palermo PA, Sicily
- **Phone:** +39 091 688 7111
- **Email:** reservations@avis.it
- **Website:** (http://www.avis.it)
- **Price Range:** $40 - $120 per day, prices fluctuate based on vehicle availability and booking advance.

4. Europcar

- **Location:** Catania Fontanarossa Airport, Catania
- **Phone:** +39 095 348125
- **Email:** reservations@europcar.it
- **Website:** (http://www.europcar.it)
- **Price Range:** $35 - $150 per day, influenced by seasonal demand and type of car.

5. Hertz

- **Location:** Via Notarbartolo, 14, 90141 Palermo PA, Sicily
- **Phone:** +39 091 630 0111
- **Email:** info@hertz.it
- **Website:** (http://www.hertz.it)
- **Price Range:** $45 - $200 per day, includes economy to luxury options.

Each of these companies offers a variety of rental options from economic models for budget travelers to premium vehicles for those seeking more comfort or luxury. Additionally, many of these agencies provide optional add-ons such as GPS navigation systems, child seats, and additional driver options to cater to your specific travel needs. Always ensure to book in advance, especially during high season, to secure the best rates and availability. Furthermore, be sure to review and understand the rental agreement, especially concerning insurance coverage and fuel policy, to avoid any unexpected charges.

Guided Tours: Options and Recommendations

Exploring Sicily through guided tours offers a profound way to connect with the island's rich history, vibrant culture, and stunning landscapes. Guided tours not only provide structured insights into the most fascinating aspects of Sicilian life and history but also ensure that visitors gain a deeper understanding and appreciation of what they are experiencing, thanks to the knowledge and expertise of local guides.

Types of Guided Tours in Sicily

1. Historical and Archaeological Tours: Sicily is a treasure trove of ancient ruins and historical sites. Guided tours of places like the Valley of the Temples in Agrigento or the ancient theatres of Syracuse offer detailed historical context provided by expert guides, who can bring the rich past of these sites to life. These tours are invaluable for understanding the historical significance and the architectural brilliance of ancient civilizations that once thrived on the island.

2. Cultural and Culinary Tours: For those interested in the culinary delights and traditional crafts of Sicily, there are tours that focus on food and culture. These might include visits to local markets, cooking classes, wine tastings in local vineyards, and workshops on traditional Sicilian crafts like pottery and ceramics. These experiences not only enrich your understanding of Sicilian culture but also engage you in hands-on activities that are both educational and enjoyable.

3. Nature and Adventure Tours: Sicily's diverse landscapes make it a perfect destination for nature lovers. Guided tours can take you on hikes through the rugged terrains of Mount Etna, boat trips around the beautiful Aeolian Islands, or bird watching in the Vendicari nature reserve. These tours are led by guides who specialize in local ecology and can provide insights into the island's natural history and biodiversity.

4. City Tours: Walking tours of major Sicilian cities like Palermo, Catania, and Taormina are excellent for those who wish to dive deep into the urban culture and historical layers of these bustling centers. Guided city tours often focus on architecture, history, and significant landmarks, along with stories that capture the essence of Sicilian urban life.

Recommendations for Choosing Guided Tours
Look for Local Expertise: Opt for tour companies or guides who are natives of the region or who specialize in specific areas of Sicilian history or culture. Their firsthand experience and knowledge enhance the authenticity of the information provided.

Check Reviews and Credentials: Before booking a tour, check online reviews and testimonials from previous participants. This can give you an idea of the quality of the tour and the level of satisfaction among past guests. Additionally, verify the credentials of the tour company or the guide to ensure they are recognized and accredited.

Consider Small Group Tours: Choosing small group tours or private tours can offer a more personalized experience. These tours allow for deeper interaction with the guide, which can be especially beneficial if you have specific interests or questions about Sicilian culture and history.

Sustainability and Respect for Local Culture: Select tours that emphasize sustainable practices and respect for local communities and environments. Responsible tourism helps preserve Sicily's unique heritage and natural resources for future generations. Guided tours in Sicily can significantly enhance your travel experience by providing structured exploration, expert insights, and deeper engagement with the island's diverse attractions. Whether you are marveling at ancient ruins, tasting local delicacies, or hiking through stunning landscapes, guided tours ensure you receive a rich, informative, and memorable introduction to all that Sicily has to offer. Here are some highly recommended guided tour companies in Sicily, offering a range of experiences from historical explorations to culinary adventures. Each company is known for its reliability, deep local knowledge, and excellent customer service, ensuring that you get the most out of your Sicilian journey.

1. Sicily Historical Tours
- **Location:** Via Vittorio Emanuele, 351, 90134 Palermo PA, Sicily
- **Phone:** +39 091 743 5006
- **Email:** info@sicilyhistoricaltours.it
- **Website:**(http://www.sicilyhistoricaltours.it)

- **rice Range:** $50 - $150 per person, depending on tour length and content. They offer a comprehensive range of tours focusing on the rich history and archaeology of the island.

2. Taste of Sicily - Culinary Tours
- **Location:** Piazza Carlo Alberto, 95131 Catania CT, Sicily
- **Phone:** +39 095 328 6138
- **Email:** bookings@tasteofsicilytours.com
- **Website:**(http://www.tasteofsicilytours.com)
- **Price Range:** $100 - $250 per person. These tours offer a deep dive into Sicilian cuisine with market tours, cooking classes, and vineyard visits.

3. Etna Nature Tours
- **Location:** Via Etnea, 290, 95131 Catania CT, Sicily
- **Phone:** +39 095 286 5120

- Email: contact@etnanaturetours.com
- Website: (http://www.etnanaturetours.com)
- Price Range: $60 - $200 per person. Explore the natural beauty of Mount Etna and surrounding areas with expert guides who specialize in geology and natural history.

4. Palermo Walking Tours
- Location: Piazza Verdi, 90138 Palermo PA, Sicily
- Phone: +39 091 848 0223
- Email: info@palermowalkingtours.com
- Website:(http://www.palermowalkingtours.com)
- Price Range: $20 - $80 per person. These city tours are perfect for those interested in diving into Palermo's vibrant culture, architecture, and history.

5. Aeolian Adventures

- **Location:** Via Porto Levante, 98050 Lipari ME, Sicily
- **Phone:** +39 090 988 0248
- **Email:** info@aeolianadventures.it
- **Website:** (http://www.aeolianadventures.it)
- **Price Range:** $150 - $300 per person. Offers boat tours and cultural visits to the stunning Aeolian Islands, focusing on local history and natural beauty.

These tours not only provide guided experiences but also respect the principles of sustainable tourism, ensuring that your visit contributes positively to the local community and environment. Booking a tour with any of these companies will enhance your understanding of Sicily's cultural and natural heritage, making your trip an unforgettable experience.

Useful Apps and Websites for Travel in Sicily

Embarking on a journey through Sicily can be a delightful and seamless experience with the aid of specific mobile apps and websites designed to enhance your travel experience. These tools are essential for navigating through the region's diverse landscapes, understanding local customs, arranging transportation, and ensuring you get the most out of your Sicilian adventure. Here, we'll explore some of the most useful apps and websites that any traveler to Sicily should consider.

Apps for Navigation and Transportation

Google Maps: An indispensable tool for both first-time visitors and seasoned travelers, Google Maps offers comprehensive map data and navigation for Sicily. Its features include real-time GPS navigation, traffic conditions, and route planning for driving, walking, biking, and public transportation.

Rome2Rio: This app provides detailed options for getting from one place to another using various modes of transport. It's particularly useful for planning longer journeys across Sicily, showing you bus, train, and ferry routes, along with estimated travel times and costs.

Language and Communication

Google Translate: While many Sicilians speak some English, especially in tourist areas, having Google Translate can help bridge any language gaps. The app supports text translation in many languages, voice translation, and even image translation via camera — perfect for reading menus or signs.

WhatsApp: Widely used in Italy, WhatsApp facilitates easy communication with local service providers, such as tour guides, accommodation hosts, or new friends. It's essential for sending messages, making voice calls, and sharing images or locations without incurring SMS fees.

Local Insights and Travel Tips

TripAdvisor: This platform remains a valuable resource for reviews and recommendations on places to eat and stay, as well as things to do. The TripAdvisor website and app host a wealth of user-generated content that can assist in making informed decisions about where to visit in Sicily.

Weather and Environment

AccuWeather: Reliable weather forecasts are crucial when traveling to Sicily, where the climate can vary significantly between coastal and inland areas. AccuWeather provides detailed weather reports and alerts, helping you plan your activities according to the local weather conditions.

Culinary Exploration

EatWith: Experience authentic Sicilian cuisine by dining with locals. EatWith allows you to book meals prepared by Sicilians in their homes. It's a fantastic way to connect with local cultures and enjoy home-cooked meals.

TheFork: A leading restaurant app in Europe, TheFork offers the ability to discover and book top-rated restaurants in Sicily. It often features special offers and provides user reviews and ratings to help you choose the best dining experiences.

Cultural and Historical Learning

SicilyCulture: This app focuses on the cultural and historical aspects of Sicily, offering insights into the island's archeological sites, museums, and historical landmarks. It includes information on visiting hours, ticket prices, and upcoming cultural events.

Additional Useful Apps

WeatherPro: Given Sicily's diverse geography, which can lead to varied weather conditions, having a reliable weather app like WeatherPro can help you plan your daily activities. The app provides detailed weather forecasts including temperature, rain probability, and wind speed, which are crucial for scheduling outdoor activities like beach visits or hikes.

Duolingo or Babbel: To enhance your interaction with locals, a basic understanding of Italian can be immensely helpful. Apps like Duolingo and Babbel offer quick lessons that are easy to digest, perfect for learning basic phrases and vocabulary during your travel. These lessons can be particularly beneficial for understanding menus, road signs, and basic greetings.

XE Currency Converter: Managing finances during international travel is made easier with XE Currency Converter. This app provides live exchange rates and allows you to calculate prices in your home currency, helping you keep track of spending and avoid confusion during transactions. Each of these apps and websites offers unique functionalities that cater to different aspects of travel planning and execution. By integrating these digital tools into your travel routine, you can enhance your understanding of Sicily's geography, culture, and history, making your visit as enriching and smooth as possible.

CONCLUSION

This enchanting island, positioned in the heart of the Mediterranean Sea, offers an array of experiences that surpass its modest size. From the historic avenues of Palermo and the intricate baroque architecture of Catania to the serene landscapes of the Sicilian countryside and the pristine waters along its coasts, Sicily invites travelers to dive into a unique mix of cultures, history, and natural splendor.

Throughout this guide, we have uncovered the key elements needed to plan and enjoy a trip to Sicily. We've provided in-depth insights into the island's attractions, from UNESCO World Heritage Sites to secluded spots away from the usual tourist paths. We've explored the rich palette of Sicilian cuisine, which reflects the island's lively history and cultural interactions. Additionally, we offer practical advice on accommodations, transportation, and navigating the island, ensuring every visitor can maximize their visit, whether they seek luxury, adventure, or cultural immersion.

Customizing your Sicilian adventure to match your interests, whether it's through historical exploration, culinary pursuits, arts and culture, outdoor activities, or rest and wellness, makes for a deeply personal and unforgettable experience. By interacting with locals, participating in the island's festivals and traditions, and adopting sustainable travel practices, you not only enhance your own experience but also help preserve Sicily's heritage and natural beauty.

Sicily presents a kaleidoscope of experiences, each component a story, a taste, or a memory to be uncovered. This guide is your gateway to embark on this exploration, to discover, and to fall in love with Sicily's allure. Whether you're meandering through ancient streets, swimming in turquoise waters, or savoring the warmth and hospitality of the Sicilian people, your journey here promises to be a remarkable adventure. As you turn each page and explore each location, remember that the true spirit of Sicily is found not only in its places but in the spirit of discovery, connection, and appreciation for this gem of the Mediterranean.

Made in the USA
Coppell, TX
26 February 2025